DREAMING HEAVEN

DREAMING
HEAVEN

The Journeybook

Gini Gentry

Lee McCormick

Francis Rico

Kelly Sullivan Walden

Agape Media International

Agape Media International
Los Angeles, California

Published by
Agape Media International, LLC
5700 Buckingham Parkway
Culver City, California 90230
310.258.4401
www.agapeme.com

Distributed by
Hay House, Inc.
P.O. Box 5100, Carlsbad, CA 92018-5100
(760) 431-7695 or (800) 654-5126

Hay House USA: www.hayhouse.com®
Hay House UK: www.hayhouse.co.uk
Hay House Australia: www.hayhouse.com.au
Hay House South Africa: www.hayhouse.co.za
Hay House India: www.hayhouse.co.in

DREAMING HEAVEN
The Beginning Is Near
Gini Gentry, Lee McCormick, Francis Rico & Kelly Sullivan Walden

Executive In Charge Of Publication: **Stephen Powers**
Editor: **Kelly Sullivan Walden**
Copy Editor: **Carol A. Rosenberg**
Design & Graphics: **Ted Raess, Raess Design**
Cover Photos: **Allan Welch**
Author Photos: **Gini, Lee and Francis by Alan Welch; Kelly by Anna D'Geami**

Motion Picture Production
Directed by **Dana Walden & Straw Weisman**
Executive Producers: **Iva Peele and Lee McCormick**
Producers: **Straw Weisman, Lee McCormick and Dana Walden**
Original Score by **Dana Walden and Philippo Franchini**
Editors: **Paul Kelleher and Blake Harjes**
Written by **Elio Zarmati, Lee McCormick and Dana Walden**

The authors of this book do not dispense medical advice or prescribe the use of any
technique as a form of treatment for physical, emotional, or medical problems, without
the advice of a physician, either directly or indirectly. The intent of the authors is only to
offer information of a general nature to help you in your quest for emotional and spiritual
well-being. In the event you use any of the information in this book for yourself, which is
your constitutional right, the authors and the publisher assume no responsibility for your
actions.

Printed on recycled paper.
ISBN: 978-1-4019-4424-7
Library of Congress Cataloging-In-Publication data available upon request.

Dedication

To life.

A special thanks to

TIME

for having been so generous in offering so much of itself to the creation of the Dreaming Heaven Experience

Contents

A Note from Kelly . . .

For those of you (like me) who live by the motto: "Leap first and build your wings on the way down," you may wish to skip past this page and free fall headfirst into the introduction. However, for those of you who would like grounding information before you hurl yourself into this book, then you'll appreciate the following facts:

1. You should know everything in this book is real, based on true events and experiences in a mystical place known as Teotihuacán, Mexico, "The place where Men become Gods."

2. This book was born in response from feedback we received during *Dreaming Heaven* (the movie) screening focus groups. Over and over we heard: *"I wished I could've paused the movie during key moments to take time to process my feelings and thoughts"; "I'd love to go to Teotihuacán to experience this journey first hand, but, due to time and financial restrictions, I can't right now"; "I wish there was a way to bring the initiates' journey from Teotihuacán to me. It would be great if there was a workbook that could elaborate on the wisdom and activations touched on in the movie, so that my community and I could not just be entertained and inspired, but transformed."*
    This is exactly what we did!
    With this book you now have in your hands, along with the DVD of *Dreaming Heaven,* you can pause the film during key moments and have guidelines to support you in a deeper exploration. It's the closest thing there is to bringing Teotihuacán to you.

3. Even though this book is a companion to *Dreaming Heaven* (the movie), it stands alone. Don't worry if you haven't yet seen the movie. However, I promise, you will want to watch it once you're about five

pages in.

4. You will hear four distinct voices throughout this journey. The first voice you will hear is mine (Kelly Sullivan Walden). For all intents and purposes you can think of me as your traveling companion, narrator, and guide to this experience. The lion's share of the book, however, embodies the wisdom of Toltec Naguals (shamans), Lee McCormick, Gini Gentry, and Francis "Rico" Hayhurst.

5. There are exercises (Activations) in each chapter's Weekly Practices, to help you embody the wisdom. In addition to the Activations you will discover journaling prompts, contemplations, and suggestions for ways to experience this process with a Dreaming Heaven Group.

6. You can experience this book any way you'd like, however it was designed with the intent to be read in 12 weekly increments so you have time, space, and wiggle room to absorb the information . . . and thus be transformed by it. You can also read this book in the following ways:

From cover to cover, as one would read a novel.

To receive guidance, as in oracle, by thinking of a question and flipping to a "random" line on a "random" page.

As part of a weekly Dreaming Heaven Group.

In weekly or monthly installments with your Dreaming Heaven Group or book club.

7. Regardless of your spiritual or religious orientation, if you are even slightly open-minded, this content can help deepen your connection to your sacred path.

8. Oh, yes, if you have fears of death, dying, or of facing and embracing the Angel of Death, you might want to stop here and pretend you never saw this crazy book.

Who Are We Really?

Introduction

The most important kind of freedom is to be what you really are.
You trade in your reality for a role. You trade in your sense for
an act. You give up your ability to feel, and in exchange, put on
a mask. There can't be any large-scale revolution until there's
a personal revolution, on an individual level. It's got to happen
inside first.

—JIM MORRISON

Our lives are built on stories upon stories, masks upon masks.
We live out each day in a personalized virtual reality equipped with
billowing smoke and ornate mirrors on the stage of a grand theatre we
call "life." Miracles and magic are possible in every moment, yet most of
us invest our faith in stories that describe our limited perception rather
than reflect our infinite potential. But what if we are more than the
stories we tell, the roles we play, and the masks we wear?

Shakespeare said, "All the world's a stage, and all the men and
women merely players . . . " and the Bible (Matthew 9:29) reads, "As you
believe, so it shall be done unto you." What if *we're making our lives up
as we go along, based on our beliefs and the stories we tell?*

And why, if we have a say in the matter, do we continue to play
the role of *victim*? Perhaps the reason is that by acting out these tragic
tales and wearing these well-crafted masks, we've simply been drinking
our own Kool-Aid. We've accepted our roles as fact . . . when in truth
they are nothing more than our own urban legends.

Most of us never consider that we are limitless beings. Instead
we relate to ourselves as one of the mere players Shakespeare mentions.
As Henry David Thoreau said, men "lead lives of quiet desperation" and
go to the grave with their song still in them. Yet, in the theatre of life—

preposterous as it may seem—we are the director, producer, playwright, and lead actor. We are even the one who controls the floodlights of our perception! If we could peek behind the backstage curtains, we would discover a great secret: **We are Divine Beings dreaming the dream of our humanity.**

For many, many generations now, we have lived life playing small and in fear. Don't you think we've suffered enough? Don't you think it's time we step up and take total responsibility for our lives? Don't you think it's time to wake up?

It's your life, your story, and your virtual reality—dream it any way you desire. But know, from this moment forward, yours can be a dream of struggle and strife, or it can be a dream of *Heaven*. We are creating every day with every choice we make, whether or not we are aware of it. I hope you will choose to explore the magic and go on a ride of epic proportions!

So now what? How do you do this? Where do you begin?

As your destiny would have it, this book is dedicated to helping you discover that you are more powerful than you could have ever fathomed in your wildest, out-of-the-box imagination. These pages form a roadmap with words as alive as you and me—brimming with wisdom, tangible exercises, activations, and contemplations that, when applied, offer a transformational opportunity to re-weave the fabric of your life.

Kelly

Before we dive into this exploration, allow me to introduce myself. I am Kelly Sullivan Walden, and I will be accompanying you on this journey. Some call me "Doctor Dream." I am a dream enthusiast of both the night and daytime varieties and I know a thing or two about masks. Throughout my life—and in particular throughout my twenties as an actress in Hollywood—I wore whatever mask, played whatever role, and tap danced to whatever song you wanted, to make you smile, convince you to cast me in the part, or prove I was worthy of your love.

That worked great for a while. I booked a lot of roles: big parts in small films, like the leading role in *Death By Dialogue*—have you seen it? Didn't think so. And I was in small parts in big productions like *Bird* with Clint Eastwood, *Leaving Las Vegas* with Nicolas Cage, and *ER* with Anthony Edwards, to name a few. I had the time of my life doing this . . . until I didn't. I found myself an inch away from becoming another Hollywood casualty. For all the parts I landed, there were hundreds more I didn't get. All the rejection sent my self-esteem into a downward spiral, and, as my life force weakened, I realized I was dying from the "disease to please."

Unlike most humans on the planet who run screaming from the angel of death, I found myself running *toward* her at breakneck speed, begging her to take me. I couldn't get the mantra out of my head: *"I need to die . . . get me off this planet."*

I didn't learn until later that I was suffering from *soul loss*. Some people experience soul loss due to trauma, shock, or a tragedy that befalls them (e.g., rape, war, sudden death of a loved one, divorce, a natural disaster). And some people are simply and irresistibly drawn—like a moth to a flame—to situations laden with emotional land mines programmed to destroy their self-worth. My soul wasn't taken from me . . . I was the pimp on the street corner selling it to the highest bidder. Because I didn't value my authentic feelings—much less my internal compass—my soul became disgusted with me and left the scene of the crime.

> There's nothing more insidious, more crazy-making, and more pathetic than a people pleaser doing every trick in the book (back flips, baton tosses, fan kicks) to please someone and fail to win their approval. You don't have to be Shakespeare to recognize a recipe for tragedy.

Without going into all the gory details, suffice it to say I believe nervous breakdowns are highly underrated, because they can, as in my case, lead to a breakthrough that initiates one's spiritual journey.

Like many of us, I turned to healers, therapists, churches, psychics, gurus, hypnosis, Tarot, Astrology, the Kabbalah, the I Ching, Reiki, past-life regressions, out-of-body projections, astral travel, chakra balancing, crystals, aura alignment, sweat lodges, meditation, fasting, chanting, yoga, trance dancing . . . and more. I even did an eight-year stint in AA (Alcoholics Anonymous) only to find out that I wasn't an alcoholic! In each of these experiences I discovered an element, a clue, a remnant of the true me behind the mask.

Through all of this, I began to feel my soul gradually, slowly, incrementally migrating back to me. A patient suitor, I let my soul know I was serious about wooing it back. I had to prove I wasn't going anywhere. Over time it began to ease back into my body, and I could feel myself breathe again. Not the shallow breaths you take when you are dog paddling through life, but the deep belly breaths that are proof your soul is finally returning.

At this point I received an invitation to go to Teotihuacán for a spiritual journey. I felt ready for my soul to come all the way back home, unpack its bags, and kick off its shoes once and for all—which is exactly what happened. If something as glorious as that can happen to me, then it's possible for you, too.

I'm of the belief that if I discover something truly wonderful and soul edifying, I must share it. I've found that if I keep an elixir to myself, it eventually loses its punch and has diminishing returns. However, when I share the magic and miracles I find along the way, they tend to multiply and grow more potent over time. So, for purely selfish reasons, I am thrilled to share with you the life-altering, mind-boggling, and soul-restoring experiences and insights I learned and earned along the journey to what we affectionately call *Teo* (short for Teotihuacán).

We cannot hold a torch to light another's path
without brightening our own.

—BEN SWEETLAND

My prayer is that you, too, will—in the reading of this book and by participating in the "Weekly Practices"— have a mask-melting experience and step out from behind the smoke and mirrors of lack and limitation into the clarity of who you are, *really.*

To help me share this experience with you, I've invited Toltec Masters Lee McCormick, Gini Gentry, and Frank Hayhurst to lead you along the journey. They are three brilliant Naguals, featured prominently in the movie, *Dreaming Heaven*, so you are in good hands.

"What's a Nagual?" you ask. I like to think of a Nagual

(pronounced "na-wall") as "no wall," which is exactly what they do; they help you to drop the walls that keep your light out, that separate you from the divine and the sunlight of your true being. That's my personal experience of them. A Nagual is "a man or woman of power; a shaman; a Toltec wisdom-keeper."

Throughout this book, Lee, Frank, and Gini will take you by the hand and lead you through the hot spots along the journey of Teotihuacán, sharing with you the ways in which you can take this inward trek from wherever in the world you are. I will be your traveling companion along this magical expedition, supporting you in calling your soul back home to your body, turning your drama into phenomena, and discovering the most glorious person you will ever meet: your authentic self.

Sound good?

Then let's get started!

Suggestions for a Successful Journey

Suggestions for a Successful Journey

Freedom isn't the goal of the journey . . .
it's where the journey begins.

—Krishnamurti

Most journeys you embark upon, whether they are physical or metaphysical, come with fanfare and accouterments, which weigh down your actual or virtual knapsack. Not so with this one. The majority of what you will be asked to do throughout this process is *unpack* who you thought you were, *drop* the heavy baggage of your false identities, and *release* the fears that have prevented you from living a life of freedom and joy.

The only thing you'll be asked to carry with you is:

Courage to inhabit the question, *"Who am I really?"*

Perseverance to continuously take action to deepen the rediscovery of who you are.

An open mind & heart to consciously guide your actions.

Willingness to live life in alignment with your deepest truth.

You may also wish to pack a Dreaming Heaven Journal (a.k.a. *Book of Dreams*—more about that later) to track the progress of your journey: the highs and lows, breakdowns, and breakthroughs.

If you choose to travel solo, *hats off to you.* However, many people find that joining forces (either physically or virtually) with a Dreaming Heaven Group adds juice to the experience—not to mention accountability, camaraderie, and support.

Rules of the Road

The only people for me are the mad ones, the ones who are mad to live, mad to talk, mad to be saved, desirous of everything at the same time, the ones who never yawn or say a commonplace thing, but burn, burn, burn like fabulous yellow roman candles exploding like spiders across the stars.

—JACK KEROUAC, ON THE ROAD

If you are the rebellious type who doesn't like to be told what to do, then you've come to the right place, and the first thing you should know is, *there are no rules.* We strongly encourage you to follow the wisdom of your heart and to listen to the voice of your inner knowing each step of the way. However, if you enjoy a bit of structure to support you as you (and your group) find your groove, then this next section is for you.

The transformational excursion laid out in this book follows the ancient Toltec path of initiation from Teotihuacán. The roots of this mystical tradition predate the ancient Mayans. In the past, this process would take years, and in some cases, initiates would devote their lives to the practice.

In modern times, most of us don't have the luxury to spend months or years immersed in the training, so contemporary Toltec guides typically lead initiates on an intensive journey over a five-day period. These intensives are often repeated many times, allowing the initiates to deepen into the wisdom at a pace that's right for them. However, in order for you and/or your group to get the most out of this experience from the comfort of your own home or community, this book has been laid out in a **12-week format**. Each section will support you in exploring one important aspect of the training per week.

Toltec initiates go out into their lives in the middle of their training and return to re-immerse themselves when they feel they are ready. This format will support your group in considering that option as well—to go at your own pace.

Teotihuacán is a living reflection of the Toltec Mystery Tradition. It is composed of plazas, pyramids, and temples; each energetically reflects the wisdom stored in its location. In each section of this Journeybook, you will hear the voices of the three Toltec guides as they express their perception, experience, and insights regarding each plaza, pyramid, or other point of interest along the path.

At the beginning of each chapter, you will find a **Word for the Week**, which has a particular significance in the Toltec tradition and is related to that week's lesson. It will be helpful to investigate the feeling tone of the word in order to understand its relationship to your life. You can deepen your experience by using the word as a mantra, an inquiry, and/or a portal of discovery for the week.

At the end of each chapter, you will discover **Weekly Practices** that can be done solo or with your group to bring the experience of the Teotihuacán journey to life in your mind, heart, body, and body of affairs. The four aspects of the **Weekly Practices** include:

Activations—Exercises to support you in embodying the core wisdom of the teaching.

Book of Dreams Journaling Prompts—Stream of consciousness writing suggestions to explore in your journal or *Book of Dreams.*

Contemplation—A meditative thought for you to marinate in and consider throughout the week, designed to raise your level of perception and awareness.

Affirmation—A simple phrase to percolate upon throughout the week, to inform your thoughts, and to realign your ever-expanding and liberating point of view.

Preparing
for the Journey
of a Lifetime

Preparing for the Journey of a Lifetime

WEEK 1

Even if you are on the right track, you will get run over if you just sit there.

—Will Rogers

Word for the Week: Perception

Most people understand the word *perception* to mean an observation or awareness of the elements of their environment interpreted in the light of their experience.

However, the ancient Toltecs saw perception as a personal mythology based on the random selection of an arbitrary point of view.

We are all slaves to our perception based on our version of reality. We select evidence which we then justify using our subjective way of seeing the world. If we take responsibility for our way of constructing "reality," we begin to garner our perception from wisdom.

Kelly

As I was preparing for the journey to Teotihuacán, I remember feeling particularly triggered on a "soul-ular" level by a question Gini asked me, "What do you most stubbornly defend?"

"Ha!" I thought, "How dare you assume there is any part of me that would stubbornly defend anything?"

I then heard my inner voice of reason quote Shakespeare's *Macbeth*, "Me thinks the lady doth protest too much."

Okay. Perhaps my slight defensiveness was a red flag calling out the fact that I believed something needed defending . . . which meant on a deeper level, I doubted the validity of the thing I was defending, or I would not need to defend it. In my case, I was defending something so basic, so core deep that it's embarrassing to admit: the fact that **I am inherently good.**

Having invested hours, years, and decades in defense of *my goodness* means, by definition, I believed I was inherently bad, flawed, *not* good. On a core level, I'd taken to heart every real or perceived rejection or criticism I'd ever received (hundreds of moments in my personal history—none more than during my most active mask-wearing days as an actress).

It was a revelation for me to examine my beliefs, to identify the cause for my defensiveness, and to even sometimes ride the high horse of righteousness. In the simple examination of this one perception, I found the space to begin unraveling the rest. As Lee says, "If you remove one brick from a wall . . . the whole thing eventually comes tumbling down."

One thing I learned is that without examining my perception, these skewed points of view will run my life. And in the examining of those thoughts, I have the opportunity to reveal the truth of who I am . . . really . . . and discover the brilliance that lies within.

On that note, I invite you to take a moment and think about what beliefs *you* defend. Take a moment and jot them down in your journal (aka *Book of Dreams*).

I now pass the talking stick to our guides . . .

Meet Your Guides

It is the supreme art of the teacher to awaken joy in creative expression and knowledge.

—ALBERT EINSTEIN

Now that we've taken care of the details, I am delighted to introduce to you the three Toltec guides who will be leading you on your journey of discovery, unraveling, and awakening.

If we searched the entire universe, we could not have assembled three more diverse guides to shine a light on your path. They come from different backgrounds and have different teaching styles (not to mention completely different hairstyles). But seriously, what these brilliantly talented Toltec Masters have in common—besides being brilliantly talented Toltec Masters—is their commitment to your freedom and to you playing your part in co-creating your version of Heaven on Earth.

What is a Toltec, and what is a Toltec Master? Great questions. You'll learn more about that in the coming pages. For now, suffice it to say they are men and women of knowledge and power trained in the Toltec mythology.

As you read this book, if you allow their wisdom into your heart, their teachings into your dreams, and their practices into your life . . . don't be surprised if in a short time you notice the story you tell becomes one that evokes the very best in you . . . and in those joining you on the stage of life. Now, let's meet your guides and discover their "stories" about who they think they are.

(Note: You'll find the guides' full bios are at the end of the book.)

Meet Gini Gentry

Gini

Hi, my name is Gini Gentry and I will be one of your guides through the magic of this journey. You're probably wondering who I am, but *which version are you most interested in knowing?*

Would you like to hear my *victim's* story of how "they did it to me" or the *hero's* tale of how I overcame huge obstacles? Would you like to hear from the *self-absorbed know it all* who was pretty sure she had the "go-to" point of view for all of life's questions or maybe the *famous Nagual Woman* who has selflessly dedicated her life to sharing the Toltec Mysteries? Wait, how about *the best-selling author* or *the girl* who waited in vain for true love? And what about *the woman* who lived with chronic pain for decades or *the bawdy female* who will do most anything for a laugh?

There have been so many me's and so many stories that I've had to ask myself over and over, "Who *am I really?*" This question propelled me along my personal journey to find out. After years of soul searching and spiritual discovery I'm delighted to hold the light for you on your personal journey to your own truth.

meet Frank Hayhurst (a.k.a. Francis Rico)

Hello. My name is Francis. It used to be Franky, then Frank, Francis, now Francis Rico . . . or Rico for short. With every name change and every accompanying incarnation I've asked myself, "Who am I *really?*" The only thing I could be sure of was that I was alive. I didn't have a clue about who I was until one day a little brown gentleman came into my music store. He was a brilliant man, but his oral tradition was spoken to the English-speaking world in broken *Spanglish*. A portable recording device was the best way to get his stories down so they could later be transcribed into good English for others to read. I helped him find the best equipment for this and in return, he helped me.

This man helped me remember back to the time in my childhood when I saw energy, when I saw through material forms, when with my grandfather's guidance I became aware of the *big picture*. I went to Teotihuacán and the floodgates of perception opened for me into the life and gifts I was born with. I was finally able to realize who I am and, paradoxically, it's still an amazing mystery. Today I am profoundly grateful to serve others and guide them in finding for themselves the truth of who they really are.

Meet Lee McCormick

I'm Lee McCormick and I am a *(fill in the blank)*-aholic. Or that's what they tried to tell me anyway. "Lee, you're an addict," they told me—a cocaine-aholic, a musician-aholic, a cowboy-aholic, a ranch-aholic, and a crazy-aholic among other things. They have always tried to tell me who I am, and I just couldn't buy it. I've done a lot of things that folks might not cotton to, but above all else I've been a human having a very large, very interesting life experience. Who am I *really*? I spent a lot of years trying to figure that one out. From playing in honkytonks, to founding *The Ranch Treatment Center,* to leading spiritual journeys to The Pyramid of the Sun, I've run the gamut, and what did I find out?

My name's Lee McCormick and I have no idea what I am, really . . . and the truth is I'm no longer concerned. Lee is the name that I answer to. It comes with quite a backstory. But you know, we're not here to talk about who I am. We're here for you to come to a greater perspective of who you are . . . *really*!

Sound good?

Then let's get started!

Welcome!

Welcome to this magical opportunity. We bring everything about ourselves along with us wherever we go. We bring our very best and our very worst. We bring all of our baggage, we bring our history, and we bring our stories. We welcome *all* of you. This journey will offer you the gift of a lifetime—it will reveal the essence and the truth of who you really are. This journey will offer you a life worth living; a life of purpose and joy; a life of peace and a life of love—in other words, a life worthy of *you*.

Gini

Welcome home! It is so wonderful to imagine you here with us; we have been waiting. This journey you are about to embark upon will be a reunion with the truth of you: the truth of your magnificence. You'll have to admit it's an exciting thought.

I remember my own experience, so I know it can be a little daunting. The good news is the guideposts you'll need are all here in the book. The key to success, however, is not the information but your own willingness. There will be great days and some not so great days. Make a habit to be kind to yourself regardless of what kind of day it is. Be open, because some of the journey will seem logical and some parts won't. When things don't make sense, go back to willingness. Let your heart take it all in. If you fall, get up as soon as you can—no recriminations. If you struggle, drop the judgment. If you're reluctant, let it be. Just keep moving forward, one step in front of the other. Love will guide the way. And we, your guides, will be here for you.

Lee

If you took a step back from your day-to-day reality and considered the immense depth and diversity of the Human experience, you'd be in awe. We live from the depths of the Amazon jungles to the tops of the Andean realms, from the deserts of the Middle East to the farmlands of the American Midwest. There are so many cultures, so many religions, histories, colors, foods, belief systems, ways of travel, styles of dress, and customs, from the nomads of Mongolia to the traffic jams of Manhattan, from the Aboriginal peoples of Australia to the royal families of England.

We each live life based on the world into which we were born. From culture and faith to families and traditions, we inherit a reality, and as we grow into adulthood, we carry our unique version of that inheritance and pass it on to our children—and their children.

This is the way of the Human, or as the Toltecs refer to it, the "Human Dream." In our world today the systems that have held us together are coming apart at the seams. Economic structures are breaking down, environmental issues are raging, religious institutions are under fire, governments are falling apart, and we are no longer able to trust people in positions of power simply because we are "supposed" to. Our collective reality is under great stress, and the world, as we have known it, is moving and shifting.

What is our reality today? What is actually *real* and what might we call real that might be better defined as virtual reality—a reality only as solid as our faith or belief in it. If we turn away from our historical and cultural beliefs, will those institutions stand? If they collapse, then how "real" were they in the first place?

We are at a great crossroads in history. From one point of view this is a tough and scary time. Our security is being rattled, as many aspects of life we had faith in are no longer worthy of our faith. If the world around us is not as we believed or as it seemed, then what is going on, *really?*

Just as we have to look more deeply at our external life, many people are also looking deeper into their personal reality—the reality that dwells within and asking even bigger questions, "If I am not what I have believed myself to be, then what am I?" "Who am I?" "Who are you?" "Who are we, *really?*"

In coming to terms with all of this uncertainty, there is one great gift: how we decide to look into the mirror of life that surrounds us and how we look deeply into our own souls. As we do this with love and self-respect, we begin to ask questions that we may have never been willing to ask . . . until now.

This is more than a simple inquiry; this is an awakening, a calling from our spirit. The truth of what we are is alive in the center of ourselves. We seek it or we don't.

Our opportunity is to awaken to authenticity—that aspect of self set in motion at the moment of conception. Our authenticity is the presence of the One that created us. It is awaiting our return to our original purpose for being in the world. This is an opportunity for grace and courage. It is an opportunity we are worthy of as children of *Life*, as children of *Creation*.

If you were to look in the mirror right now, you could see through the filters of your past stories or you could see through the lens of infinite perception. Where will you place your attention?

What is it, this thing that you call "me," this thing that I am, *really?*

Welcome to the journey of a lifetime. You have just pulled back the curtain on the Great Wizard of Oz. And if you're willing to jump in 100 percent, you might find yourself facing a far greater opportunity than you could have ever imagined.

What Is Teotihuacán?

The process that's available at Teotihuacán allows us to move in a way that divests us of illusions, so that we can get to a place where we discover something true, authentic, and real.

—FRANK HAYHURST

Kelly

The name *Teotihuacán* can be translated as "City of the Gods," or, more accurately, "The Place Where Men Become Gods." *Teo*, as the locals call it, is a vast archeological site, 30 miles northeast of Mexico City, containing pyramids and temples built in pre-Columbian America. It has long been thought of as having deep religious and spiritual meaning to its original inhabitants. The most prominent natural feature is the Rio de San Juan (the San Juan River), which runs through the center of the site, though it is dry most of the year. Its principal structures include:

The Plaza of Hell & Temple of Quetzalcoatl

The Avenue of the Dead

The Plaza of Earth (a.k.a. Temptation)

The Place of the Women

The Plaza of Water

The Plaza of Air

The Plaza of Fire

The Plaza of Recollection

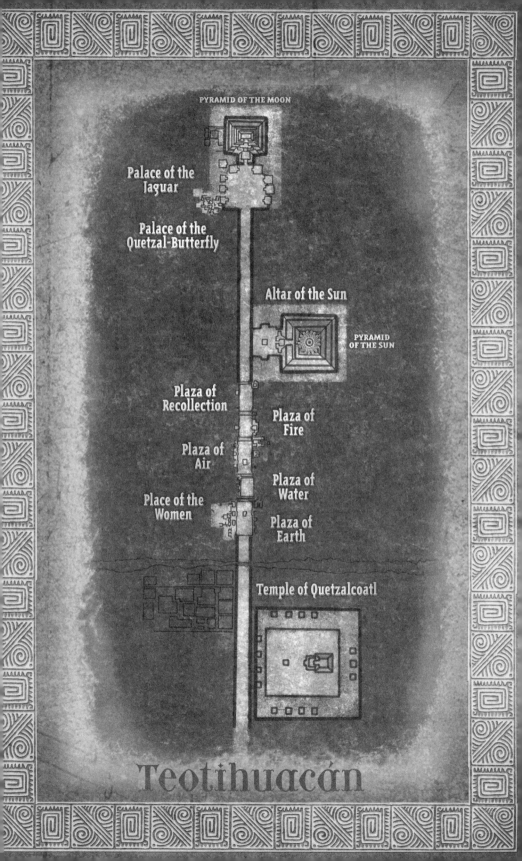

PYRAMID OF THE MOON

Palace of the
Jaguar

Palace of the
Quetzal-Butterfly

Altar of the Sun

PYRAMID
OF THE SUN

Plaza of
Recollection

Plaza of
Fire

Plaza of
Air

Plaza of
Water

Place of the
Women

Plaza of
Earth

Temple of Quetzalcoatl

Teotihuacán

The Pyramid of the Moon

The Plaza of the Jaguar (Heaven)

The Pyramid of the Sun (the second largest pyramid in
the New World)

These structures are believed to have been built between 100
BCE and 250 CE, with the city reaching its cultural zenith around
450 CE. In addition to Teotihuacán's sacred structures, archeologists
have unearthed a network of residential buildings, which housed a
population of more than 100,000, placing it among the largest cities in
the world at that time.

While the "founders" of Teotihuacán remain shrouded in
mystery, it is generally believed that the Toltec people were central to its
creation and existence. Because of its huge population, it is also believed
that Teotihuacán attracted a mix of people that included the *Zapotec*,
Mixtec, and *Maya*. Archeological evidence shows that Teotihuacán was
a center of both craft and commerce, but its most enduring legacy is as a
spiritual center.

Beyond the history and geography lesson, I figured you should
hear about Teotihuacán directly from your guides, who have been there
collectively hundreds of times (in fact, Lee and his family live part time
in Teo in a magical place appropriately named "The Dreaming House").

I asked Lee, Gini, and Frank to describe Teo and the peculiar
energy that draws people there. After all, there's got to be a reason why
it's called the place "Where Men Become Gods." Here's what our guides
had to say. . . .

Describe what Teotihuacán is and what it means to you.

Lee

There is a presence in Teotihuacán that was anchored
thousands of years ago. It's fed by the practices that have been carried
on there for all those years.

Gini

Teo is a living edifice of wisdom that offers seekers an energetic journey through the ascending levels of consciousness. Each time I take a group through the process, I think of it—and they experience it—as a reunion with the impeccable truth of our eternal nature.

Rico

There's a cave system in the shape of a four-leaf clover at the base of the Pyramid of the Sun, which has been used for 3,000 years (that we know about) as a place of healing and wholeness. An energy radiates from this place that we can only call the *divine out-breath of the origin of creation.* It is still present, saturated, accessible, strong, and alive.

Lee

Teotihuacán is a geographic location. It's a spot on the map. It's a place I consider home. It's a consciousness, it's where I woke up to the knowing that there is a lot more to reality than what I was living. Teotihuacán is the light; it's the world; it's creation; it's an ancient city; it's a consciousness unto itself; it's a living place; it's a cosmic, multi-dimensional reality; and it's a place of dirt, rocks, air, water, and spirit.

Teotihuacán is an alive place. Human energy and attention have been attracted to it for specific purposes over thousands of years. I equate it to walking into a 1,500-year-old Catholic church. When you enter, you feel an energy. You don't need to be Catholic to feel it. It surpasses belief systems. It's the same if you walk into an ancient Hindu temple or a mosque. The belief system is irrelevant. What is relevant is the faith and energy of the people who've prayed there throughout history. Teotihuacán is like that; it's "fed" by people who have gone there with open hearts, willing to interact and engage with its energy. That's what gives Teotihuacán the life that it holds today, and it stretches back through time like a thread.

Gini

We can speak about Teo from so many different levels of perception. If we talk about it from a place of limited awareness, you could say it is a ruin—an old dead site from a long gone culture. Using greater awareness, we can witness it as an amazing place where the veil between worlds is particularly thin, thus allowing a magically accelerated possibility for remembering the truth of our authentic being.

From a divine point of view, you could say it is a sacred place that offers a reunion with spirit. We have decided to call some places on the planet *sacred*. Teotihuacán is one of those places. It is all of those things, depending on what eyes we choose to look through. To me, it is foremost a mighty gateway to the dream of *Heaven on Earth*.

Rico

The first thing that occurs to me when I say "Teotihuacán" is gratitude. I feel gratitude not for a place of pyramids, a physical place of structures made of stone, or even a place that has a long history. I feel gratitude for the tremendous expansion in my life catalyzed by the mysterious presence that is Teotihuacán.

People come to Teo to experience the sacred journey from all different traditions and religions. One thing they have in common is that something deeply intriguing has called them. Even though they come from different walks of life, they hear the same call. People come to Teotihuacán when they recognize that something in their lives has got to change, shift, or improve. Problems have to be solved. They have to figure something out. Some people are in despair, but many others are simply curious and emotionally compelled. They want to find out what this experience is. Something calls within their hearts.

It's not about having a paranormal or mystical experience. It's about an authentic connection with something totally magical—the *mojo* of creation. Teotihuacán is a place where you recognize that others who have gone before us have traveled this same road. You realize that Teotihuacán has transformed people who have gone on to live blessed lives, became multi-dimensional, and found a rare and sustaining freedom. You can feel the vibrational resonances of those who have traveled the path before.

When we go through the process at Teotihuacán, it's a process of discovery—not discovering what's authentic and what isn't, but a process of discovering the misidentification and limitations we've placed on ourselves. As we divest ourselves of what we are *not,* we discover who we *are* and what we are truly capable of.

The misidentification I'm referring to compels us to forget who we really are. We think we are our bodies, our emotional responses, our thoughts. In Teotihuacán, we find out that we're not. We discover that we are flow; we're a burning fire of something indescribable, something there is no word for in the English language.

Love comes close. From the beginning of time, Teotihuacán has been the presence of the mystery. How is it possible that this place became imbued with the wildest energy of the origin of creation— the huge *Yes* that informs everything . . . including our lives and our breath and this moment? How is it that Teo, a place imbued with this energy, can be involved with us, caring for us, and assisting us in our awakening and in our evolution? It's a mystery. Teo is the real thing. It's *the* mystery.

Gini

Teotihuacán was originally envisioned as a mystery school similar to the great schools used by other traditions such as those from Egypt and Tibet. Now Teotihuacán is a place where masters guide initiates to their awakening by discovering the unconditional world that lies beyond dualistic thinking and fear. These masters have embodied eternal truth and are willing to share it with initiates committed in their search for the vastness of being.

On our journeys through Teo, one of the most important things we do is help people examine their choices; we expose the limiting choices currently impacting their lives and reveal the beliefs that are lurking behind those choices. We shine a spotlight on their unwitnessed beliefs and then point out some of the more life-affirming options available to them. The highest quality of mastery arrives through active acceptance, great love, and by moving the place of our decision making from the mind to the heart. In this way, Teotihuacán offers us an opportunity to remaster this thing we call *Life.*

Weekly Practices: Week 1—Preparing for the Journey of a Lifetime

Happiness lies in our own backyard, but it's probably well hidden by crabgrass.

—DELL CROSSWORD PUZZLES

Kelly

All of the ways your guides have described Teotihuacán are true. If you've not been before, perhaps one day you will go. However, in the meantime, allow these next pages to *bring Teotihuacán to you.* While you are reading this book, from the comfort of your home or your Dreaming Heaven Group's meeting place, know that by the power of your thought, all the plazas, pyramids, aspects, and dimensions of Teotihuacán are within you . . . and are possible to experience right where you are.

> **Suggestion:**
> **Listen to Dreaming Heaven Meditation 1, Introduction:**
> SEE PAGE 175 of this JourneyBook for instructions on how to download your prepaid copy of *Meditations from Dreaming Heaven*

Activation 1: Book of Dreams

Your first step in this journey is to create your Dreaming Heaven Journal—your own personal *Book of Dreams.* This guidebook will become a powerful resource of wisdom and illumination for your journey. The discoveries you make, the knowledge you gain, and the wisdom you embody can be shared with your Dreaming Heaven Group. The contents of this journal will form a bridge from where you are now to a reunion with your authentic self. It is private and not to be shared. This journey is sacred work, done between you and the Great Mystery.

You will be supported by your Toltec guides, empowered by the materials prepared for your use within this Journeybook, and ultimately awakened by Teotihuacán itself.

Whether your *Book of Dreams* is a physical journal (recommended), or if it lives on your computer or phone, it will become a sacred presence in your life when you initiate it by writing, signing, and dating the following declaration:

"Today, my intention is to examine my life and step away from the limiting choices, fear-based beliefs, and habitual actions that are not accurate reflections of my authentic Self. I will be completely honest with myself. I will face the truth with courage and without judgment. I make this promise in the spirit of good faith and the quest for the realization of the dream of Heaven on Earth."

_____   _____
Signed   Dated

*If you are in a Dreaming Heaven Group, take the pledge together, allowing the energy and accountability of the group to support you.

Activation 2: Talisman

Find or create an amulet or talisman that reflects your innate spiritual essence. Wear it or carry it with you during your journey as a constant reminder of the truth of your being. Allow it to interrupt your idle thoughts each time you notice it, so you can refocus your attention in the moment and remember what is enduring and real.

Throughout the day, when you "bump into" your talisman (in your pocket, on your altar, or around your neck), pay attention to your patterns of awareness. Notice if you are dreaming into the future or rehashing the past. While holding your talisman in your hand, connect with the *now* moment by sensing your feet on the ground or your legs in your seat, shifting your awareness to the present. Breathe, become still, and notice what is around you. Feel the air on your face. Listen to any sounds that caress your ears. Notice the feel of your talisman in your hand. Fill the moment with gratitude for life's gifts, learning opportunities, and the miracle of being alive.

*If you are in a Dreaming Heaven Group, bring your talisman to the group. Share about what it means to you and the ways in which it is helping you to become more present.

Activation 3: Sacred Place

Take off your sandals, for you are standing on holy ground.

—The Holy Bible, Exodus 3:5

Whether or not you've ever been to an officially recognized place of power, acknowledge that the place where you are at this very moment, on planet Earth, is a sacred place . . . because *you* are here.

Go outside, take your shoes off, and feel the earth, grass, or sidewalk beneath your feet. Envision Mother Earth supporting you.

Stretch your arms, look up to the sky, and notice everything you see as a reflection of the sacredness of life.

Lie on the ground and feel all of existence supporting the one-of-a-kind creation of life you are. Say out loud, "This is holy ground."

*If you are in a Dreaming Heaven Group go outside barefoot as a group, and explore this exercise together followed by a group discussion based on the question, "What defines sacred space?"

Book of Dreams Journaling Prompts

Now it's your turn to initiate an inquiry of self-discovery and explore the various points of view you hold about the miracle of creation you call *you*. Throughout the week you'll begin unraveling who you think you are, so that you will be able to distinguish who you *really* are. Often the most difficult perspective to observe is the one we are standing in. With that in mind, as objectively as you can:

Write the story of who you think you are (a.k.a. "The Story of You").

When you are done, read your story out loud.

Journal about the way your body feels as it listened to your story.

Look at your personal history and identify the many voices and characters who speak from within you: the well-intentioned you; the frightened you; the loving, kind you; the mean-spirited, jealous you; the vehicle of all the voices, your body; and the many other versions of you that present as roles—parent, child, partner, student, teacher, etc.

Think of your personal history and identify which stories have changed and which ones you still cling to.

Describe the lenses of perception through which you typically see life; e.g. victim, martyr, judge, victor, etc.

To access greater happiness in your life, identify what perceptions you prefer to use in place of the ones you have identified.

Tell "The Story of You" without mentioning your relationships, talents, skills, and career.

Tell "The Story of You" from the perspective of you having unlimited choices and being free to be your authentic self.

Contemplation: Wise-Being Point of View

Close your eyes and take a few grounding breaths. Envision aligning your inner perception with wisdom. Now bring to mind the wisest, most awake person you've ever read about or known, or create your own composite. Next, use your imagination and begin to feel how they perceive life and how they experience reality. Imagine that you can borrow their eyes for one hour and perceive life as they do. Open your eyes and walk through your world seeing your surroundings through the perception of this wise being. Notice how this perspective differs from your normal point of view.

Contemplate the question, "What changes would I need to make in order to see myself, the world, and the people around me as this wise person does?"

Affirmation

Today I see with the eyes of wisdom as I realize that the heaven I seek is all around me, always has been, and always will be. It is a matter of perception.

Beginning the
Journey

Beginning the Journey

WEEK 2:

It doesn't interest me who you know or how you came to be here. I want to know if you will stand in the center of the fire with me and not shrink back . . .
I want to know what sustains you from the inside when all else falls away.

—Oriah Mountain Dreamer

Settling Your Affairs

Life shrinks or expands . . . in proportion to one's courage.

—Anais Nin

Word for the Week: Fearless

Most people would define *fearless* as being brave, or at least free from fear.

From the Toltec perspective, fearlessness is equated with love. Toltecs believe Hell is the place of suffering and is ruled by fear, with fear being the absence of love, acceptance, and peace. In order to move beyond fear, stop contemplating it, and instead contemplate courage, adventure, the end of suffering—in other words, fearlessness.

Kelly

Now that we have a sense of where we are, what Teotihuacán is, who our guides are, and who we are (or not), we are ready to begin the first leg of the journey. This is where we will meet a very special "energy" called Quetzalcoatl (the winged serpent). However, before we do, we must prepare by settling our affairs.

I must admit, when the notion of "settling my affairs" was first presented to me, it set off inner alarm bells. I sat in my room in Teotihuacán writing my Last Will and Testament (as you will be led to do in the Activations at the end of this section) while shaking like a leaf. I wouldn't describe myself at this point as fearless—at all. I felt the fear and crawled on my belly along the journey anyway.

I don't know that I've ever cried so hard as I did during this exercise. (If you've seen the movie, you've seen me *boohoo* like a banshee in *The Place of the Woman,* but the tears I'm talking about here were torrential.) I wailed because I truly stepped into the place of saying "goodbye" to all my loved ones. I wrote them each a love letter in which I appreciated, forgave, and praised them. I listed my precious memories with them and acknowledged how much they meant to me.

I always fancied myself a free-flowing type that could "live and let live" while easily facing death. I had no idea how untrue that was. I never knew how attached with a Kung Fu grip I was to all people, places, and things of the 3-D world. I was shocked at the tree-trunk-sized umbilical chords I had to my husband, my sisters, my mother, father, dog, and friends. Thank God Gini's room was adjacent to mine. She heard my howls through the wall, came in, and embraced me like an angel as I sobbed.

I don't mean to scare you . . . you may truly be a free-floating "in this world but not of it" type. But even if you are attached, it's okay. "Settling Our Affairs," as strange as it may seem, is the first step to being able to live with freedom, presence, and authenticity.

I'll allow your guides to describe in more detail what "Settling Your Affairs" entails . . .

What does it mean to "Settle Your Affairs"?

Lee

When I think of settling my affairs, it means to be ready to let go of all the attachments to the entire construct of my life—and to willingly let go of it. Let go of it with sweetness; let go of it with sadness; let go of it energetically; let go of it emotionally. Settling my affairs means surrendering to the fact that nothing in this world really belongs to me anyway, so I'm settling it out. I'm settling my affairs and I'm ready for whatever is next.

Letting go of personal history is one of the ongoing practices of the teachings that have been passed down for thousands of years from the mystery school that existed in Teotihuacán. To let go of my personal history is to free myself from needing to continue to live as though this story of my history were true.

It's scary when we wake up and realize the story we're living in day-to-day life is not working for us. Questioning our reality is terrifying. We've all been taught that there's nothing worse in life than being wrong. And the reality is that when we begin to question our lives as individuals, when we begin to ask:

"What am I doing?"

"Why am I doing it?"

"What am I responsible for here?"

"What's happening with me?"

"What's happening in the world around me?"

. . . this is when everything begins to change.

There's a program we've all bought into that says, "You'd better not be wrong!"

It's time to come face to face with the truth and the reality that the life we've been living and the choices we've been making are our responsibility. The gateway to stepping into our own power as individuals is facing the fears that come up when we consider taking our power back from hell. We've given it away by being afraid of being responsible.

The idea of getting my affairs in order, of facing the Angel of Death, and of looking at my reality is a scary proposition, but it's unavoidable. To move out of our innocence, to move into our great awareness, we have to first and finally take ownership for having created our lives to this point.

We need to move out of blame and move back into self-responsibility. You have to be willing to go there . . . and get to the other side.

The first act is accepting the invitation to show up and question your life—to show up and be willing to look at yourself.

Say to yourself, "If I'm 100 percent vested in where I'm at now, for me to get from where I'm at now to somewhere else—that means some things have to be released." Then ask, "What am I willing to let go of?"

We realize we're going to have to recollect some energy. We're going to have to recollect some time. We're going to have to recollect our ability to do something new.

This is the set up for "getting your affairs in order." And looking at the proposition that in order to really move from where you're at today to another life, a new life—a greater life—there is a dying process involved.

To get your affairs in order, the first thing to do is to ask yourself, "Where am I today; what's going on with me now? Am I willing to look at the life I'm living?"

The second thing to do to bring all of this together is to make a decision, and to come to terms with the question, "Am I really willing to let it all go for the sake of living something better and greater?"

The third thing is to consider the reality that in order to move from the life I live today to a greater life, the life I live today has to die. I have to be willing to have that degree of commitment in order to free myself up, so I'll have the energy available to create a new life.

In order to have this greater life that is awaiting you, you literally have to become willing to lose your physical form. It's like disintegrating as the human and experiencing your spiritual essence, the aspect of you that is pure light.

This aspect of you is so huge, so expansive, and so free. A lot of people look at it and think, "Oh those people must be doing drugs." The fact of the matter is drugs cut you off from the ability to go there. That's my experience. You absolutely don't need drugs to find the freedom that is your birthright to experience.

Kelly

Most people think they have choice. They think they have dominion over the reality they're living in. In fact, they have very limited choices to exercise—because they have yet to discover the vastness of possibility available to them. They don't realize that, in any moment, they can choose to align their awareness with an expanded perception. They don't realize they can examine other possibilities, because they have yet to discover they exist.

Being born into this world as a human being, you're born into a legacy, a story. You're born into descriptions. You're born into a way of being that's specific to your family, your culture, and whatever's going on in your community in that place and time.

We adopt and download all that information. The human blueprint is like a computer that comes with all the programs pre-installed. However, what is different about us human beings is our consciousness—our spirit. Living the experiences of a place like Teotihuacán allows us to literally go beyond the way life (our computer's operating system) has been defined.

The Island of Safety (In the Sea of Fear—a.k.a. Hell)

Kelly

Hell. It's not the fire and brimstone place we've all heard about . . . but a place where we examine our beliefs that have kept us from a more, shall we say, heavenly life experience. In spite of its name, I came to love and deeply respect this place because it offers the opportunity to identify and release the fears and limitations I allowed to box me into a life that is less than the legacy I came here to live.

I was instructed to pick up a few natural objects (stones, twigs, weeds, etc.) to symbolize the things, thoughts, beliefs, and memories that had kept me in hell. At first I couldn't think of anything, so I walked around in a daze. Then, out of nowhere, a pointy black rock spoke to me, "I'm the boy in sixth grade who broke your heart." A curved twig yelled, "I'm your twisted ideal relationship you keep trying to live up to." A gnarled bunch of dead grass hollered, "I'm your awards and accomplishments!" A sandy brown speckled pebble whispered, "I'm the baby you think you are supposed to have but never quite make the time for." A cluster of jagged grey rocks chided, "We're the girls and women who you thought were your BFFs but who cut you down the moment you turned your back."

This went on and on as I bumbled along through the plaza, my heart more tenderized with each step. I heard the adage, "You can't heal what you can't feel," and felt reassured, because I was *feeling* all of these attachments. By the time I reached the Island of Safety, both of my hands overflowed with all of the (literal and figurative) *sticks and stones* that had weighed me down in my life . . . and I was ready, willing, and thrilled at the prospect of being able to release them all.

Allow your guides to fill you in on this process from their perspective . . .

What is the Island of Safety in the Sea of Fear?

Lee

We open the journey by inviting you to acknowledge the fact that maybe the world we're living in today has become hell on earth—even though what we were offered (and are still offered) in every moment is to live the dream of heaven on earth. It's become hell on earth for any number of reasons. Some of the most obvious are based in duality, judgment, and fear. We're constantly measuring ourselves against one another. The legacy of the humans has become overwhelmingly wounded and sad and continues to be passed on from generation to generation.

You wake up in hell, because you were born into hell. It's a legacy that exists, because, for whatever reason, we humans have been rather slow at realizing we can do it another way. We have to be willing to go to whatever lengths are necessary to die to the old dream and live a new life; a new dream.

We have an idea that our baggage is all bad stuff. The truth is that our baggage is comprised of good stuff, bad stuff, and in-between stuff. It is a culmination of energies: emotional energy, intellectual energy, judgments, opinions, and stories. It's all the energy that we've collected during the course of our lifetime. Those energies become problematic if we don't find a way to release them and let them go.

Somewhere down inside of you, you have to come to believe you are worth the time, energy, and dedication to yourself. This is between you and you. It's not between you and your boss; it's not between you and anyone else out there; it's between you and you—on the inside.

We are capable of doing this process. We've simply never been taught that we are . . . and we've certainly never been guided into it. From the perspective of our culture, this process looks weird and strange. And in our culture, we immediately think anything that looks to be too expansive is crazy or drug induced. But this process is very natural, very human, and very real. We all have the ability. All it requires is that we be willing to let go.

Having an expansive experience goes beyond what we're supposed to be able to do. Jesus walked on water, yet we think humans can't walk on water. Why are we so sure? I've had experiences in my life that were clearly not experiences I'm "supposed" to have. I've seen spirits. I've had voices talk to me. I've had all kinds of things happen. Through those experiences I became aware that reality is much bigger than what I was told.

We human beings are expansive . . . much more than we realize. Each one of us will experience reality in our own unique way depending on who we are, choices we make, and situations we're in.

Right now you are being given an invitation from Life to be who you are, to live and create a life for yourself that's a reflection of who you *really are,* and to no longer live your life trying to be what you think is expected of you. From this point forward you no longer have to spend your time living up to a story you've made up. From this point forward, you no longer have to adopt or inherit a life based on what others say it should be. Right now you have an opportunity to focus on the fact that every day you have a choice to be authentic, to be real, and to be true to yourself.

Gini

Our first stop in the vast complex of Teo is the arena of Hell where we take an inventory of the false beliefs that cause us to suffer.

Hell is home to all the things we are not: judgment, anger, blame, and betrayal. In the center of the arena, there is an island. The island represents the illusion of safety we experience when we are surrounded by our familiar world: our relationships, possessions, and accomplishments. Most of us don't realize we are trapped; surrounded by a wall of fear. Hell is a profoundly important first step in our journey, for it is here we can take responsibility for our creation of "reality" and gift back to the heart of creation our limited experience of ourselves. As we do this, we can bring wonder, awareness, and love to our ability to begin anew, with a clean slate.

The Plaza of Quetzalcoatl

I am an avatar and messenger sent at the end of a world age to bring a new dispensation for humanity—a new covenant, and new consciousness.

—DANIEL PINCHBECK

Kelly

Now it's time to meet the ancient Toltec avatar, Quetzalcoatl. At first I didn't understand what all the fuss was about regarding this "plumed serpent." However, over time, I've developed a reverence for this presence. I've learned that he/it is known as an awake being—or an awake aspect of ourselves—that we would be wise to call upon throughout this journey. Enjoy meeting this multidimensional, and extremely powerful, being.

Allow your guides to give you a bit more insight . . .

Who . . . or what . . . is Quetzalcoatl?

Lee

One of the most beautiful aspects of the indigenous cultures is that they consider all of creation to be aspects of God, the Creator. They believe in no single entity or deity, that all creation is God, all creation is alive, and all creation is conscious. They hold Quetzalcoatl in the light as having an infinite number of aspects.

Quetzalcoatl was—and still is—the avatar of the Aztecs and the indigenous peoples of Teotihuacán and Mesoamerica. The Mayans know Quetzalcoatl by another name, *Kukulkan*. To me, Quetzalcoatl is a multidimensional Christ consciousness.

In a greater sense, Quetzalcoatl is an enlightened aspect of all creation. Quetzalcoatl's awareness is conveyed through light, as is all knowledge. The consciousness of Quetzalcoatl is available to all of us, just as the consciousness of Jesus, Buddha, and any great Teacher is available to all of us.

Quetzalcoatl is the plumed serpent. The snake aspect lives closest to earth—to the body of The Mother. It is told in mythology that Quetzalcoatl woke up to the fact that he could expand with no limitation. The plumed aspect of Quetzalcoatl represents the part of him that infinitely grows, rises above earth, ascends to the heavens, and learns to fly. From this higher vantage point, Quetzalcoatl can look down on all of creation from a higher point of view than when he is on earth.

Quetzalcoatl was known as, "He who sweeps the path clean." In this way, Quetzalcoatl is also symbolized by wind, so when there's a big wind, the Toltecs believe they are in the presence of Quetzalcoatl.

The multidimensional nature of Quetzalcoatl is evidenced even in the geography of Teotihuacán, in that the Avenue of the Dead, from an aerial view, resembles the body of a snake. The Plaza of Quetzalcoatl is where we typically begin the journey because Quetzalcoatl's plaza is also known as the place of transformation and all possibilities.

The value for us on our journey is in the embodiment of our ability, as human beings, to recreate reality at will. Quetzalcoatl is the mirror for that process. As we go into the Plaza of Quetzalcoatl, we invite participants to acknowledge the fact that perhaps the world they've been living in has become hell on earth—when the dream of heaven on earth is always at hand.

When our lives become hell, it is primarily because we base our experience on a judgmental, dualistic perspective drenched in fear. We measure ourselves against one another in an overwhelmingly wounded and sad human legacy. This legacy gets passed on from one generation to the next, because most of us haven't changed the story. We haven't changed the story because we're so vested in the version of reality that we've been programmed to live as little kids—in whatever cultures we're born into.

The dream and the reality of Quetzalcoatl is offered to us so that we can transform. As in the similar stories of Jesus, Buddha, Mohammed, and Krishna, Quetzalcoatl did it for himself and for us. He showed us how by his example. All of the world's religions, at their core, offer us that same motivation: We can transcend if we are willing to take 100 percent responsibility for our lives.

Quetzalcoatl was an avatar in the Toltec culture. Quetzalcoatl is said to embody a Christ consciousness, an advanced consciousness, based on love and the transcendence of duality. Quetzalcoatl, like other enlightened beings across world cultures, led by example. Through his life he demonstrated the profound possibility for living an impeccable life.

Rico

Quetzalcoatl is an ancient symbol of an energetic reality that is almost indescribable in language. Quetzalcoatl is known as the winged serpent, which represents the integration of three different worlds: the snake that crawls with its belly on the ground, the conscious and aware living being that has relationships within the tribe, and the eagle that flies in the air. To unify these three things means something unique, different, and mysterious. It represents a form of alignment that we normally don't see.

Normally we're trapped in the underworld, going through life with our bellies on the ground. Some of us also inhabit the middle world, the world of close, connected, extended family and tribe of interconnected support and community. Rarely, some of us soar to the higher world where we have a sky-high perspective. The image of a plumed serpent means alignment with all these worlds. We could also look at the snake as representing the reptilian or metabolic part of our brain, the part that controls our metabolism and our basic life force. Quetzalcoatl represents the fact that it is possible to integrate and link our reptilian nature with our presence in community and our highest spiritual capacity. In so doing, we become capable of a multi-dimensional experience.

Quetzalcoatl is alive. It is also a potent symbol used to describe the *mystery*. When I think of Quetzalcoatl, I realize it doesn't solely exist in metaphor, analogy, or language. Quetzalcoatl exists in the realm of pure perception and is present in this moment, ready to meet you in the here and now.

Quetzalcoatl is the awakened one who moves through the matrix of life—hell—and is immune to its hooks and demands.

—Peggy Raess

Weekly Practices: Week 2—Beginning the Journey

He who binds to himself a joy does the winged life destroy. But he who kisses the joy as it flies lives in eternity's sunrise.

—William Blake

Activation 1: Settle Your Affairs

Make a list of anyone and everyone with whom you feel "incomplete." Do you owe someone an apology? Is there someone you need to forgive? Are there amends you need to make? Is there someone to whom you need to say, "I love you"?

Once you've completed your list and identified what it would take to become "complete" (at peace) with the people on your list, begin to take the actions needed to put these relationships in good standing, so that you have no unfinished business and no regrets. You can do this by making actual contact or through meditation or journaling. If you need to complete with a person who has passed away, you can communicate your thoughts in a letter. Read the letter aloud to their spirit and burn it when you are done.

Do you have a Last Will and Testament? If not, make a list of your possessions and where you would like them to go when your time on the planet is through.

*If you are in a Dreaming Heaven Group, after each member does the above Activations, take turns allowing each member to share their experience, feelings, and reflections regarding "settling their affairs."

Activation 2: Mirror, Mirror

Step in front of a mirror. Take a breath and center yourself in your heart. Then gaze into your eyes, and make a commitment to your journey by saying the following aloud:

I am willing to honestly look at my life.

I am willing to question myself without judgment.

I am willing to see if my beliefs support who I really am.

I am willing to question the reality I've created for myself.

I am willing to let go of who I thought I was in order to become free . . . in order to become the true "me" I was born to be.

*If you are in a Dreaming Heaven Group, each member should pair up with another member and take turns expressing the above phrases while looking deep into the eyes of their partner.

Activation 3: Recall, Review, Release

Fear rules hell, but hell only exists in the mind, and the mind is the world of illusion. Knowledge describes the illusory way humans dream the story of hell. When we pursue knowledge, we get an even larger description of a skewed reality, and it holds us back. However, unlike knowledge, *wisdom* leads us forward. To get back to our innate wisdom, we need to rid ourselves of our fear and judgment. This exercise offers the doorway out of hell.

Write an exhaustive list of the fears that limit your happiness and trap you in hell. For example, look at the fears that create scarcity, anger, jealousy, apathy, betrayal, cynicism, or other emotional suffering.

Set aside 15–30 minutes and find a quiet, private space where you will be undisturbed. Close your eyes and begin to notice your breathing. Allow your breath to become deep, full, and audible. As you breathe, intentionally exhale fear, discomfort, criticism, and distraction.

With each inhale, breathe in love and peace. Now you are ready for the Activation.

Recall: Pick one of the fears on your list. Become willing to see, feel, or remember where this fear first made its appearance in your life.

Review: Impartially scan this image and each subsequent image and feeling that arises in your awareness. Disengage from attachment and judgment, and trust the images that appear.

Release: With each exhale use your breath to return any energy (criticism, blame, etc.) you carried forward that was not yours. Use your inhalation to pull back any energy of your own that you left at the scene. If you bring back fear (or any other negative energy), send it down through your arms and into the earth. After your release is complete, surround the scene with acceptance. Once you are complete with one fear, release the image and move to the next one on the list. When you are finished, offer a prayer of gratitude.

*If you are in a Dreaming Heaven Group, do this exercise together—each person picking a fear from their list and running it through the "Recall, Review & Release" formula at the same time. Make sure to build in time for participants to share their breakthroughs and *ahas* with the group.

Activation 4: Lay Your Burdens Down

We've heard that heaven is all around us. Why don't we see it? Why does the world look like such a tenuous and precarious place? To find the answer at the root of this perception, we need look no further than the arena of Hell.

In the middle of Hell there is an edifice that is distinguished by its solid structure. It is known as the Island of Safety. The mythology of the Island of Safety is that we erected this formation in response to our domestication. In other words, to maintain an illusion of security, we keep a small (confined, limited) space to live our lives. We create our Island of Safety in an attempt to protect us from what seems very much like an ocean of fear surrounding us. This place offers us an illusion of control, but we have confused *safe* with *familiar*. Because the unknown frightens us, we stay stuck in our limitations. But to embark on the journey, we have only one choice: we must leave the island and successfully cross the ocean of our fears.

Write down on a piece of paper the fears that keep you in suffering on your Island of Safety. Hint: examine your relationships, your employment or school choices, your life situation, your frustrations, your painful emotions, your self-doubts, and your heartbreaks for clues. Beneath these life circumstances, you'll find the fears that perpetuate your suffering.

To represent the Island of Safety, find a bandana, large cloth napkin, or other basically square piece of fabric that measures at least 12 by 12 inches. We will call this piece of cloth a mesa (Spanish for table). It will eventually become your personal altar (a sacred space that you create as an open doorway into communication with the Divine Mystery). For now it represents what you have created in your life up to this point. Your cloth represents the Island of Safety that is located in the Plaza of Quetzalcoatl. In order to meet Quetzalcoatl—the feathered serpent—and successfully enter into the transformational process of Teotihuacán, you must acknowledge and release the fears that keep you trapped in Hell.

Lay your cloth on the ground—being outdoors is best, but indoors works too.

Take a 30–60 minute meditative walk. Pick up small stones, shells, small sticks, or whatever you'd like to represent the fears you uncovered in your contemplation. You may also gather items that represent your opinions about why things are the way they are in your life, along with any limiting points of view.

In order to leave the Island of Safety and enter Teotihuacán aligned with Quetzalcoatl's energy, we must identify and release the fears at the root of our suffering. Whatever fears we carry forward will hamper our ability to align our journey with the uncompromising honesty and unconditional love of Quetzalcoatl.

Hold the rocks, sticks, and shells you have gathered in your hands, and know that you hold the fears that have contained and limited your life. Set this burden down on your cloth, take a slow, deep breath, and state out loud, "I'm done!" You are declaring that you will no longer allow your fears to control your life in the interest of your supposed "safety."

*If you are in a Dreaming Heaven Group, instruct everyone to arrange their cloths in a circle. Take the stones, shells, and twigs they have gathered. The group witnesses as, one at a time, each person stands in awareness of the burden they carry, and states, "I'm done!" and sets their attachments on their mesa, thus releasing their burden.

Book of Dreams Journaling Prompts

Throughout the week, journal your answers to the following questions:

What role has fear played in your life?

How have you allowed fear to define you?

Can you recall moments in your life when you have demonstrated fearlessness? If so, describe them. Who would you be, what would your life be like, if you were *fearless*?

Contemplation: Initiation

Think of a time when you were afraid. Bring the experience into present time and feel it now. Allow the feelings to intensify. Become aware of what happens to your breath. Notice what your inner critic says to you. In the midst of the fear, notice what about you is untouched and unchanged. What is at the root of the story? What is deeper? What did you have to tell yourself to make the fear real? If you remove the pictures, what is left?

We resist change because we confuse it with who we are. Release the identification once and for all.

Imagine you have laid your burdens down, crossed the ocean of fear, and begun to ascend the face of the pyramid of Quetzalcoatl. Imagine with each step that you deepen into extraordinary strength. The feeling of freedom overtakes you.

You are now standing atop the pyramid of Quetzalcoatl, looking into the open heart of this being of enlightened consciousness. Become willing to entrain to this energy, to embody its presence . . . and to be embodied by it. In an act of pure courage, bravery, and willingness to become forever free of fear, connect with your commitment to this journey. Now, leap across the divide in the center of the pyramid into the great unknown wellspring of infinite possibility to affirm your intent.

Affirmation

I am a fearless, timeless, ageless being of light, love, and courage.

Crossing
the River

Crossing the River

*Until one is committed, there is hesitancy, the chance to draw
back . . . Concerning all acts of initiative (and creation), there is
one elementary truth the ignorance of which kills countless ideas
and splendid plans: that the moment one definitely commits
oneself, then Providence moves too . . .*

—W. H. MURRAY

Word for the Week: Attention

Most people associate the word *attention* with a state of
alertness or readiness; or perhaps someone or something toward which
to give, pay, or direct our energy.

The Toltecs believe we are constantly bombarded by people and
things that hook our attention. To follow the initiate's path, we have to
hold dominion over our own attention. In order to cross the point of no
return—the San Juan River—we must pass our first test and convince
the *Angel of Death* that we have dominion over our attention.

Kelly

Colleen, a willowy brunette woman from my group with
other-worldly hazel eyes, was called on to portray the Angel of Death.
As I waited in line to approach her at the San Juan I tried my best to
mentally prepare for this bizarre encounter. I recalled a therapist once
telling me, "Kelly, there are many people within you. Think of these

53

sub-personalities as participants in a wild parade. The goal of therapy is to get the entire parade marching in the same direction."

As I stood in line to meet the Angel of Death, my parade was a jumble and my attention was everywhere but present. How could I be present when I was trying to corral all my scattered sub-personalities? A heroic part of me marched forward, fearlessly leading the pack. A terrified little girl aspect lay curled up in a cave, closing her eyes, waiting for this scary journey to be over. A tough-girl part of me stood on guard to punch the lights out of any authority figure (even the Angel of Death) who might hurt my feelings or threaten or intimidate me. I could feel the teacher's pet aspect of me just wanting to get it right so as not to get into trouble and to show everyone how *good* I was. I breathed deeply and called my motley crew together as best I could. Then, with the courageous part of me taking the lead and summoning the attention of the rest of the parade, we looked directly into the surprisingly warm eyes of the Angel of Death. She nodded her head, giving me (we) permission to cross the Rio San Juan.

Now it's time for you to take a deep breath, call your parade members to order . . . and pay *attention* to the guides as they lead you across the Rio San Juan . . .

What does it mean to "cross the river"?

Rico

You've just let go of your fear and attachments to what you mistakenly believed kept you safe. You've met Quetzalcoatl; and in meeting this avatar of divine presence who displays the alignment possible within us, you've begun to perceive a new possibility for yourself. Now, at the river's edge, you must decide, "Do I dare cross to the other side?" To evolve, to transform, to grow, you simply must cross the river.

Lee

Throughout human mythology there are very important, powerful, significant rivers, like the Ganges, the Amazon, the Nile, and the river Styx, that separate the above world from the underworld. When you come to the San Juan River, you'll find it to be a place of reckoning, a place to contemplate whether or not you really have the staying power to pursue this journey. You'll find this to be a place to decide whether or not you have the energy or wherewithal to make it through to the other side. Because once you've crossed that river, you go into no man's land . . . and there is no going back.

Once you cross the river, you're still wrapped in the construct of everything you think you know. You have your masks, identities, stories, knowledge, all the things you've accomplished, and memories of all the times you failed. You don't cross the river clean. You cross the river still carrying all your baggage and all your suitcases. The cleaning process, however, begins immediately after crossing.

When you prepare to cross the San Juan River, you must come to a great place of commitment within yourself. You give your word that you are going forward. And when you do, you set a powerful energy in motion. At the river you begin to gain awareness . . . and your life will never be the same. When you cross the river, you must be strong in your intent—resolved that you're going to go the distance. If you aren't strong, you'll be pulled back into your familiar version of hell. The gravitational pull of familiarity is stronger than we realize. It takes great resolve to walk across the river, away from hell, as there is often a huge pull to stop, go back, and stay in the comfort of the life you have always known.

Before you can cross that river, you must come face to face with the guardian of the river, the presence we call the Angel of Death. Even though this passage is guarded by the actual reality and presence of death, in the Toltec tradition we call this presence an angel, because we don't see it as a fearsome, frightening, horrifying being out to get us. We see the Angel of Death as an advisor and an ally who has something important to share with us.

If we can release our fears long enough to hear what the Angel of Death has to share with us, then we are permitted to cross the river. However, if we don't hear, or if we *refuse* to hear the Angel of Death, then we keep struggling with our fears and our suffering; and we go back to hell. I've seen many people get turned away at this point. The only way we can cross the river is to become present with the Angel of Death and accept her gift, her message, and her presence at the threshold of our journey into authenticity.

Lee

When you cross the river, you're literally stepping into the unknown . . . you don't know what your life is going to look like on the other side. Nobody does. You can have all the intentions, plans, and expectations you want. However, reality is what it is—and our projections are what they are. The two may not have anything to do with each other.

Meeting and Befriending the Angel of Death

That nothing is static or fixed, that all is fleeting and impermanent, is the first mark of existence. It is the ordinary state of affairs. Everything is in process. Everything—every tree, every blade of grass, all the animals, insects, human beings, buildings, the animate and the inanimate—is always changing, moment-to-moment.

—Pema Chodron

Gini

You can say, "I love this sweater," but in fact it belongs to the Angel of Death . . . and someday she will reclaim it. Just as it is with all of the things in this world, they are all dust to dust.

To play with the Angel of Death, you must invite complete respect for her dominion over life's fragility. If you are willing to accept the fact that the Angel of Death can come and reclaim everything you've become attached to in the material world, and if you are willing to release your attachment, then she is delighted to be of service to you. When you do this, you have an opportunity to truly be in this world without being mired in your attachments.

For me, the Angel of Death has become this amazing

benefactor. I play with her in my life and have had experiences with her that replace fear with absolute wonder. After all, it's only fear. What if we say, "Come, fear, come and play with me"? We can just as easily say, "Come, love, come and play with me." We say, "Come, Angel of Death, and let me give you my fear." And she says, "Okay, I'll take it. Let's play."

The ideal relationship with the Angel of Death happens when we say, "My beloved, may I present to you my emotional body, so that I can go find out the truth of who I am? May I give you these emotions that come from fear? May I even give you the emotions that come from love? May I give them all to you? I am on a quest to find what is true, so that I may come back in service to love."

What we're doing is learning to walk with the Angel of Death. As we do, we return our false sense of ownership back to her stewardship, so that we can have an experience of the pure essence of ourselves.

Rico

Meeting the Angel of Death prepares us to cross the river. She encourages us to take this journey, to which probably any sane person would say, "What? Face death? Face the reality of the end of everything I am, everything I know? No way!"

Of course this is not something we want to do willingly. Before we're able to consider meeting the Angel of Death, we need to know what we're up against—our biggest fear. As a species we are hardwired for survival, and the idea that we would willingly face our death only occurs in the case of extreme heroism, where someone does something spectacularly risky to save another's life.

When we behold death as an advisor and ally, we are reminded that every moment is precious. This moment is irreplaceable. This moment is a profound gift. Be alive here in this moment. With the Angel of Death by our side, there is no place for petty grievances, frustration, or jealousy. In the presence of death we are reminded of the preciousness of the moment.

If the Angel of Death sees that we cherish the moment; that we embrace the truth that everything is alive; that we recognize love as the founding, guiding, illuminating, joyful essence of divinity that is the gift of our lives, then she allows us to pass.

For death is the destiny of every man;
the living should take this to heart.

—Ecclesiastes 7:2

Weekly Practices: Week 3—Crossing the River

It is not the strongest of the species that survives, nor the most
intelligent, but the one most responsive to change.

—Charles Darwin

Having released our fear in the living, loving presence of Quetzalcoatl, we are now ready to cross the river—the point of no return—into the energetic process of Teotihuacán. The guardian of the river, the one who either allows us to pass or refuses our passage, is the Angel of Death, whom we must face, so that she may ascertain our commitment.

The Angel of Death holds sway over the material world. Change is the constant of our universe, and the Angel of Death is the agent of change. We think it is natural to resist change for all we're worth, but we must surrender to the Angel of Death our resistance and what we have known in order to see what is true and enduring in the gift of our life.

Suggestion:
Listen to Dreaming Heaven Meditation 2, Crossing the River:
SEE PAGE 175 of this JourneyBook for instructions on how to download your prepaid copy of *Meditations from Dreaming Heaven*

Activation: Meeting the Angel of Death

Go outside in nature, to a beach or to a yard, preferably a place where you can touch the earth. Draw a line on the ground representing the river of no return. Stand on one side of the line, approximately six feet away, with an awareness of the life-changing commitment you are about to make.

Envision the Angel of Death standing as the threshold guardian on the other side of the line—a place that represents your liberation and freedom. Feel, envision, or imagine that you are walking towards the Angel of Death.

With each forward step, deepen into your courage and willingness to offer her your attachments, so you will have no obstacles between you and your reunion with your authentic nature. Take a final step and stop directly in front of her. Imagine you are looking into her eyes. She sees if you are ready, and you will intuitively know her answer. If she allows you to pass, open your hand and hold it palm forward, with your fingers up, as a symbolic gesture to anchor your intent to cross over. If the Angel sees fear and avoidance and refuses to allow you to pass, strengthen your resolve by gently breathing in and out to center yourself. Then, exhaling and releasing any residue of fear, when you are prepared, approach the Angel again.

*If you are part of a Dreaming Heaven Group, appoint someone to be the Angel of Death. A line is marked on the ground. The person selected to represent the Angel stands behind the line while everyone else in the group stands single file on the other side of the line, facing the line and the Angel of Death. Each person proceeds, one at a time, to the line and then stops. Take turns facing the Angel of Death and looking into his or her eyes.

When the Angel of Death feels that each participant is sufficiently willing and ready, they are given a nod of approval—a sign to cross over. Once you've crossed the line and moved past the Angel of Death, you've symbolically crossed the San Juan River . . . and the journey is on!

Transforming Your Relationship with Death

Another way you can do this with your group is to:

Divide the group into pairs facing each other. Each pair stands three feet apart.

One person represents the Angel of Death and strikes a fierce, threatening pose, while the other person cowers—struggling, attempting to fend off the inevitability of Death.

With a show of great courage, the person facing Death ceases struggling, and lowers their hands into a gesture of welcoming recognition and acceptance of the presence of the Angel before them.

In this moment of magical potential, the person inhales and exhales, then sharply exhales, breathing out their intent to cement the new relationship.

The Angel of Death then walks around the person, approaching them from behind, and speaks over the person's left shoulder, "In my presence, recognize that this moment is precious. This moment is all you have. There is no time to waste on petty grievances, anger, jealousy, envy, frustration, or despair. This moment is a gift. This moment is sacred. This moment is your opportunity to live a life worth living. This moment is yours to live, without fear."

After one half of the group transforms their relationship to the Angel of Death, the pairs switch roles and enact the same ritual.

Book of Dreams Journaling Prompts

Throughout the week, journal your answers to the following questions/prompts:

How does it feel to have made a great and powerful commitment to wake up?

How might it serve you to have the Angel of Death as your ally and mentor?

With the Angel of Death in your awareness, what might you lose? What might you gain?

What would you and your life be like if you were willing to make complete peace with your own death and pay 100 percent attention to the miracle of life around you?

Contemplation: Where's Your Attention?

Find a comfortable place in the outdoors. With your eyes open, take 3–4 long, slow breaths. Become deeply aware of your surroundings. Where is the sun? Can you feel its warmth on your face? What colors do you see? What do you smell? What sounds do you hear? What do you feel with your sense of touch? Can you feel the air on your face and the ground under your feet? How do you feel emotionally and energetically? Bring your full attention to this moment. Notice the tug-of-war within your mind wanting to contemplate thoughts and feelings outside this moment. Bring your attention back to this place and this time. Do this for about five minutes several times a day.

Affirmation

This moment is a profound gift. It is irreplaceable. I am alive, present, giving my full attention to the preciousness of this now moment.

Then you will know the truth, and the truth will set you free.

—JESUS, QUOTED IN JOHN 8:32

The Plaza
of Earth

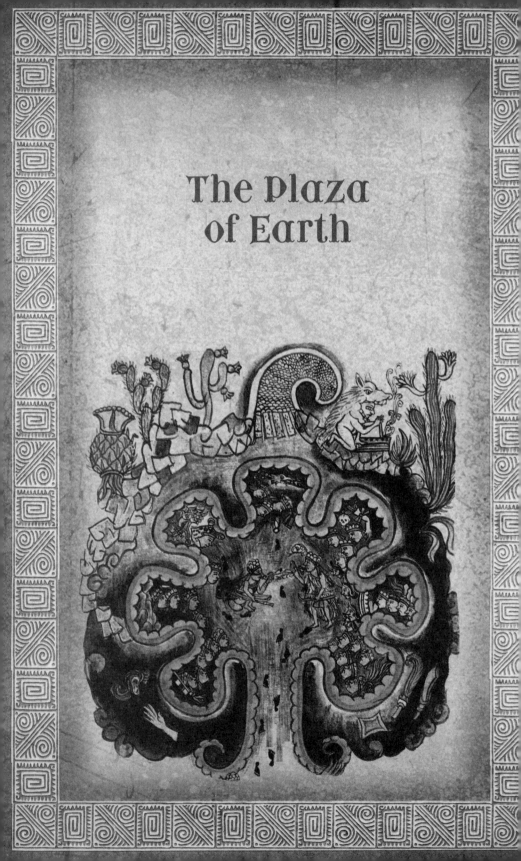

The Plaza of Earth
WEEK 4

"Nothing really dies," I told him. "It just turns into something else. Everything is always changing form. Do you remember the pumpkin that rotted into the earth in your garden? Tomatoes sprouted where it used to be. This bird will go back to the earth and turn into lavender flowers and butterflies.

—ANNE CUSHMAN

Word for the Week: Life

The typical point of view about the meaning of the word *life* is vitality; being in touch with an animating energy; or simply the opposite of death.

According to the Toltecs, life is a miracle. It is only when you make peace with death that you can truly be present to the miracle of life. In the Plaza of Earth, we give up our attachment to ourselves as a body, so that we may truly live and have the life that is our birthright.

Kelly

In the Plaza of Earth, we give up our attachment to our physical body. In the western world, so many of us women (some men, too) would say, "Good riddance!"

I was one of those westerners. When I was younger, I got so caught up in fashion magazines, having absorbed the myth that my legs should look like pencils. No matter how much I starved myself, I remember thinking, "I HATE my thunder thighs!" I had to swallow the bitter (diuretic) pill that even after fasting, dieting, and running for miles with my thighs constrained in Saran Wrap, I was never going to look like supermodel Elle Macpherson . . . so I rejected myself on a daily basis.

Then I stood in the dirt of the Plaza of Earth, faced with the task of saying "goodbye" to my physical body, and I started feeling the tiniest glimpse of remorse:

Hey, wait a minute . . . I kind of like this body . . . it's not so bad. I'm not quite ready to give it up. Even though it never looked the way I thought it should, it has been relatively healthy, functional . . . and even beautiful in its own interesting way.

I heard the song "Big Yellow Taxi" by Joni Mitchell playing in the background of my mind, *Don't it always seem to go, that you don't know what you've got till it's gone . . .*

What a shame! What a bummer! What a loss to have not spent more time appreciating my physical vehicle—regardless of the fact that it was never going to be a size two. Instead of starving it, hating it, wrestling it into clothes that were too tight, hiding it behind clothes that were too loose, berating it, and feeling burdened by it like a cursed albatross, I could have been celebrating the millions of daily miracles that happen within every cell, atom, organ, bone, tendon, and tissue of this living, breathing, one-of-a-kind phenomenon that is my body.

I felt ridiculous for having treated it so poorly for all those years. I vowed, if given a chance, to make it right. In the blazing heat of the Teotihuacán afternoon sun, I scurried around the Plaza of Earth with a vengeance, collecting rocks, twigs, and as many purple wild flowers as I could find, and created the most beautiful altar to my body known to man (or at least to any Toltec strolling through the Plaza of the Earth that day). I found a pinkish, smooth rock to represent what I formerly called a flesh bag, but now knew as the Divine's work of art. As I laid "my body" down gently into the soft ground, I wept with gratitude for it, praising it, asking it for forgiveness, and ultimately . . . releasing it. Your guides will take it from here. . . .

What do you mean by "release the body"?

Rico

The first plaza you reach after crossing the River—the line of inevitability of your journey—offers the opportunity to recognize you are not your body. Here in this place of gravel, dirt, and stone, we return to the earth something that has been a precious gift from the earth: our bodies.

Gini

Our first delicious encounter with the Angel of Death in the Plaza of Earth offers us the opportunity to release our limited attachment to and identification with the body. It is a beautiful, even joyous, experience to create and attend our own funeral. Setting a strong intention and going in with great consciousness offers us a wonderful opportunity to make peace with our own physical transition.

Lee

The Plaza of Earth represents the physical body. It represents our physical form. And it is the place where we look at the relationship we have with our physicality.

Earth is the element that corresponds with our physical body, as it literally contains the elements that make up our physical bodies. Our body is born of the earth—born through our human mother. The elements that comprise humans are earthly elements, which is why so many indigenous people hold the perspective that the earth is the mother.

Rico

Here in the Plaza of Earth you also have an opportunity to forgive yourself and others who have injured your physical vehicle. Typically forgiveness has a moral connotation. However, from a shamanic point of view, it's simply a very practical matter. Return energy that's not yours, so that you are no longer compelled to carry it. When you can surrender your body to the earth, be aware that along with it goes all of the injury you've been holding.

The Plaza of Temptation

Gini

The Plaza of Earth is also known as the Plaza of Temptation, simply because you are just barely out of Hell and can still see it like a ghost haunting you off in the distance. The pull is still very strong. It is important to keep focused on where you're going, not on where you've been.

Rico

This is also the point where we look back at our life—at what we thought we were. The Plaza of Earth can be a place where you will be tempted to turn around and hightail it out of there. However, if you allow yourself to experiment as you create a burial and memorial service for yourself, you will recognize you are not your body.

Once you do this, you may discover you are something else. Who you are—who you really are—is still present. After seeing your own burial and hearing all of the kind things said about you and what kind of a person you were, you begin to realize that you really are not your body.

Let's say you had 200 arms, and they were all full of attachments to people, places, things, and beliefs—everything that keeps you feeling safe and secure. Now imagine you release all the baggage being carried by your 200 hands, and set your burdens down. When you do that, you create an energetic vacuum. The experience of temptation is the habitual desire to pick those things up again. Before our burial we felt burdened by all that we were carrying. But now that we've laid our burdens down, we miss the security in the familiar experience of carrying the weight of the world along with us. Oddly, this made us feel secure when we thought we were our bodies . . . and now that we are free from that burden, we're empty handed and can feel very insecure. However, with open hands, an open heart, and open eyes, we are ready to take the next steps on our journey.

Gini

To be able to remember the essence of ourselves, we must move everything aside to see what is true—to discover what endures and is eternal about our nature. The Plaza of Earth is a wonderful place to begin to let go of what we are not.

Is the physical vehicle—the physical essence—the truth of who we are? The only way to know is to begin to release. When we bury the physical vehicle (or our attachment to it) we release it back to the Angel of Death for safekeeping. It is on loan from her, after all, and by all rights it's hers.

We have to see what we are not. For example, we've been taught that our body is who we are. When we came into form, we were given this whole download, that was already present in the collective belief system for eons, of what it was to be human—what is was to be in a dualistic belief system based on fear.

Rico

Ultimately we realize there is no temptress tempting us. What is tempting us is our own recognition that we're in unfamiliar terrain, that we're not using the props we gathered around, and we aren't in the same old story that we've told a thousand times about the creation of our lives. Here we are with nothing in our hands (in fact, no hands at all) feeling the call to be tempted back to the familiar . . . but we don't heed the call. We continue ascending through the belly of the serpent.

Weekly Practices: Week 4—The Plaza of Earth

Do not stand at my grave and weep. I am not there. I do not sleep.

I am a thousand winds that blow. I am the diamond glints on

snow. I am the sunlight on ripened grain.

I am the gentle autumn rain.

Do not stand at my grave and cry. I am not there. I did not die.

—Anonymous

In the previous week, you met and forged a new relationship with the Angel of Death. You crossed the river of no return and committed to releasing your attachments so you could uncover your authenticity. Here in the Plaza of Earth, you meet the Angel of Death again to surrender your attachment to your body. These Weekly Practices are designed to allow you to discover that you are not your body but something mysterious and eternal.

> **Suggestion:**
> **Listen to Dreaming Heaven Meditation 3, Plaza of Earth:**
> SEE PAGE 175 of this JourneyBook for instructions on how to download your prepaid copy of *Meditations from Dreaming Heaven*

Activation 1: Preside Over Your Funeral

Find a private space, and gather a pen and paper, so you can prepare your eulogy. Write this story from the point of view of a loved one who could witness the gift of your life—your contributions, accomplishments, what and who you loved, and the story of those that loved you.

When you are finished, go outside in nature. Find a rock, crystal, or shell to represent your body. Dig a hole in the dirt or sand. Place "your body" in the hole and read your eulogy out loud. Imagine your family or friends gathered to say goodbye. Say a few words of appreciation for the body that is now departing from the mortal coil. Honor your body by placing a flower or stone on top of your grave.

*If you are in a Dreaming Heaven group, let the members of the group represent your family and friends as you say farewell to the life you knew. If you like, you may also invite them to speak.

In privacy respond to the following questions (you can do this silently, out loud, or in writing in your *Book of Dreams*):

What kind of care did I take of my physical body? What was the relationship that I had with my body?

Did I live in judgment of my body, or did I celebrate and appreciate it?

How would I treat my body if I had another chance? What did I accomplish in my life?

Did I follow my heart's desire? Did I love fully?

What did I leave undone that I would change if I had another chance?

*If you are in a Dreaming Heaven Group, go out in nature and allow time and space for each member of the group to conduct their funeral. Upon completion, allow each member to share their experience, insights, breakthroughs, and revelations.

Activation 2: Write a Letter to Your Body

In your *Book of Dreams*, write a letter of apology to your body, recognizing the ways you have been disloyal to your closest, beloved life companion. Promise in writing to cherish, honor, and care for your body from this point forward.

Sit alone in front of a mirror in a darkened room, and with a single candle lighting the scene, read your apology aloud to yourself. Then, read it aloud again, holding your focus on your commitment to transform your relationship with your body.

Book of Dreams Journaling Prompts

Journal throughout the week about your answers to the following questions:

How has the fear of death kept you from fully living?

Who would you be if you fully inhabited your life?

After having "buried your body" how do you feel about it now?

What actions will you now take to nurture and sustain your body as the temple it truly is?

Contemplation

Find a quiet place where you will not be disturbed to lie down and close your eyes. Use your breath to still your mind. Allow your imagination to come forward and transport you to the day of your actual funeral. See yourself lying on a flat surface. You can hear voices talking around you, but it is too late. There are no second chances—your life is over. Even with your eyes closed, you begin to see a field of light entering your awareness, and you become present. The voice of the Angel of Death emerges from the center of the light. This energetically exquisite being extends her hand. Fearless, you offer no resistance. She asks you to gaze deeply into her eyes, so you will recognize her when she comes for you. This is not the time. She has come only for your attachment and to offer you another chance to do it differently. She offers to relieve you of your burden, and you give it willingly. As she fades into the light, she offers you a secret: you are not your body, you are the mysterious life that eternally animates your body. Offer her your gratitude. Sit up and cherish the freedom of no longer carrying the burden of the thought, "I *am* my body." Sway, dance, or move your body in celebration of having been loaned the gift of the body you call yours for a bit more time.

Knowing now that the Angel of Death has given you an extension, a little more time with your physical body, what will you do differently? What actions will you take? Notice your inner dialogue about your body. How is it different than it was before your "funeral"?

Affirmation

I proceed today with full appreciation for my body temple— and for my very life.

Place of the Women

Place of the Women

Mother is the word for God on the lips and hearts of all children.

—James O'Barr, The Crow

Word for the Week: Peace

Most people hold *peace* as being a state of tranquility, quiet, security or order.

Toltecs hold *peace* as being the essence of our true nature. The goal of this part of the journey is Forgiveness—peace being the byproduct. The Toltecs believe that when we forgive ourselves and everyone else for absolutely everything, our mind is no longer pulled in two. When this happens we can drop vengeance, pain, and resentment, and return to our birthright: peace.

Kelly

We tend to minimize—I know I did—the impact of the role our mothers played on our development as humans, as well as on our ability to trust life. I recall reading a statistic published in *Psychology Today* (allow me to paraphrase) stating that even the best mothers only get it right 60% of the time. Yet, as babies, we are completely dependent on them. Russell Farrell wrote the lyric, "The first cut is the deepest." And for many of us, that cut happens with the feminine face of God, otherwise known as our mother. In the Place of the Women, we are embraced and immersed in the unconditional love of The Mother, redeemed in our relationship with the sacred feminine, and ultimately healed and set free to love with an open heart.

One of the questions people ask me after they've seen the *Dreaming Heaven* movie is, "Why were you crying so much in the Place of the Women?"

My answer often starts out a bit defensive (Gini would say it's my attempt to keep my "cool card"). "I'm normally not *that* emotional. I cry when I'm sad or touched by something beautiful . . . but normally I'm pretty even-keeled."

So, why did I let it completely rip in the Place of the Women? All I know is there is something about Teotihuacán and the permission given on a journey like this . . . especially in this place where women gathered in ceremony, ritual, rites of passage, and healing. In this womb-like cavern, I felt embraced by profound safety and love, and I was given the once-in-a-lifetime opportunity to release shards of pain . . . that I didn't even know I'd been carrying. I intuitively felt that the Place of the Women could handle what no human could hold for me.

I felt permission to be the healthy version of *La Llorona*, the weeping woman depicted in children's stories as a frightening character that grieves for her dead child. I wept my heart out for the children I hadn't yet been able to carry to term in this life, and for all the women— past, present, and future—who have or would ever experience an excruciating loss. Here, in the Place of the Women, in the well that leads to the heart of the Great Mother—knowing she knew what to do with it—I gratefully released my sorrow.

It was also a privilege to create a "tunnel of love" for the men to enter the Place of the Women (as seen in the movie) as a way to embrace them energetically as they entered this place of forgiveness. To look at their faces as they entered and see these strong, macho men as innocent little boys before the great mother touched my heart.

Now the guides will take you by the hand and escort you into the Place of the Women. . . .

Tell us about the Place of the Women.

Kelly

The next stop on our journey home is the temple of the Divine Mother, called the Place of the Women. The women in ancient days came to this sanctuary to receive counsel from the wise women, to have their babies, and to commune with the Great Mother.

In the Place of the Women, we are invited to experience our own reconciliation and reunion with the sacred form of the deep feminine. Many of us may have had challenging relationships with our birth mothers and may have felt abandoned by the nurturing presence we so desired. In turn we abandoned ourselves or sought *fool's gold* substitutes for the mother-love for which we hungered. When we go into the Place of the Women, we go to rectify our feelings of disconnection and abandonment and, with forgiveness for ourselves and everyone else, reopen our hearts.

In the Place of the Women, we realize the heart of the Great Mother was always with us. We were never alone or abandoned, but, because we had placed our attention on the illusion of our pain, we had not witnessed the truth that the Great Mother was with us all the time.

Rico

When we talk about the Place of the Women, we aren't talking about "male" and "female" on this planet. We could call this place the temple of "She who birthed all of creation into manifestation," or "He who is birthing all of manifestation perpetually every moment," or "For we who are being birthed continually in this flashing radiance of illumination that is Life itself."

Thank goodness, too, because we benefit immeasurably from the fact that creation is ongoing rather than static. The gift of this place is that we can release our connection with the patterns, routines, habits, and addictions of our normal life, and instead, discover this place of rebirth and renewal. Here with the cosmic mother of it all is the place where we can go to find the essence of ourselves and remember our connection with the sacred.

In this place, women lead the way . . . and it is so beautiful and important that we recognize the sacred within the feminine. Women have an evolutionary edge on men. In many ways they are sharper, smarter, stronger, more sophisticated, more gifted, more constant, and more present. Just the fact that women give birth gives me a profound appreciation for them.

In the Place of the Women, a gift awaits the women who go there. The opportunity for them is to divest themselves of the inauthentic beliefs about what a woman is. They can reconnect with the depth and the truth of the divine feminine . . . and remember that *she* is within. The women who visit this place are a gift to The Mother . . . as much as She is a gift to them.

The opportunity for men is to enter into this place with a willingness to come clean, with forgiveness in their hearts, and a willingness to stand in the presence of women with integrity and total presence—without grudges, resentments, or misunderstandings. In the Place of the Women, in the presence of the feminine, the opportunity for men is to be in total integrity and impeccability.

The Plaza of Water

Do you have the patience to wait till your mud settles and the water is clear? Can you remain unmoving till the right action arises by itself?

—Lao Tzu, Translated by Stephen Mitchell

Kelly

In the Place of the Women, I'd shed so many tears that by the time I entered the Plaza of Water, I was ready to release all attachment to my emotions. I must say, I didn't shed a tear in this plaza . . . in fact, quite the opposite. I danced, twirled, and played like a dolphin in water, ecstatic to finally feel back in the flow of life.

In the Plaza of Water, I got to explore the purity of my emotions . . . and I got to see where I'd "worked it," so to speak (like the times I'd turned on the waterworks to get out of a speeding ticket).

I got to explore my "emotional addictions"—like the habitual Rebel/Submission roller coaster that goes a little something like this:

"Get me out of here, I need space! Wait a minute, where are you going? I didn't mean it . . . sorry . . . let me make it up to you. Ok, it's getting hard to breathe in here . . . get away from me. Oh, sorry to offend, really I don't need so much space . . . I really want to be closer, not further away . . . "

Here in the Plaza of Water I could see for the first time that I have my drama-go-round, emotions, and addictions . . . but they don't have to have me. It's so beautiful, it makes me want to cry. Before I do, I'm passing the talking stick, once again, to your guides . . .

What is the opportunity for us in the Plaza of Water?

Gini

Once we've experienced the Place of the Women, it is fluid, natural, and easy to then go to the Plaza of Water, a great expanse that represents the emotional body. In this Plaza we have the opportunity to offer the fearful emotions we have been carrying to the Angel of Death, so we can be free to experience emotions that are born from our birthright of love.

So many of the emotions we've been circulating have been burdensome. We've been profoundly impacted by fear-based thoughts and emotions in spite of our birthright of wholeness.

In the Plaza of Water, we get to ask the question, "What is true?" Do the emotions we experience come out of conscious choice or reaction? Do our emotional responses come from fear or love? Do we know the difference?

The only way we can know for sure is to say, "Angel of Death, my beloved, may I present to you my attachment to my emotional body, so that I can discover the truth of who I am? I have confused who I am with the emotions I am experiencing. Take this from me, because I am on a quest to find what is true. Take it from me, so that I may come back to the service of love."

Lee

The Plaza of Earth is where we release our physical body. The Plaza of Water is where we release our emotional body. Water corresponds with emotion. When emotions come up, often there are tears. Once again, we are given the opportunity to have a reckoning with the nature of our relationship with our emotions. As aware, awake, adult human beings, we have a responsibility for how we hold ourselves in relationship with emotion. In the Plaza of Water, we explore the questions:

Do you indulge in your emotions?

Are you conscious and responsible for your emotions?

Do you live in judgment of your emotions? Do you let emotion pass through you?

Or do you judge and project your version of reality onto others based on whatever emotion you are experiencing in the moment?

What's the true nature of your relationship with emotion?

Emotions are a natural aspect of life. Emotions come up during the course of human experience, and if we are in touch with our feelings, we will have an experience that produces an emotional response. Have you ever considered that you have a relationship with your emotional responses to life?

Emotional energy is a power we feed on psychologically, intellectually, and physically. For example, if someone is a *rage-aholic*, they will literally develop an appetite for the energy of anger. It's a big and powerful energy. People that rage a lot will create situations where they can get angry, because they need that fix. It's like a food or a drug; they crave the energy. The only way to shift this is to develop an awareness about it—to look at yourself and become willing to see beyond the justification of your mind.

Are any of these emotions authentic?

Gini

They're all real in that we experience them, but they aren't all a reflection of our authentic nature. With awareness we learn to discern the difference between emotions that come from fear and emotions that come from love. We tend to suffer in response to our fearful emotions. We don't want to experience them, and that thought keeps them from moving through us, so then they get lodged.

Rico

In the Plaza of Water we explore the genesis of our emotional fears so that we can become conscious of their presence and disempower them. Our ultimate goal is to live our lives authentically, making our decisions from the "brain" of the authentic self, the heart.

In the Plaza of Water we continue to discover our misidentifications—for example, "I feel, therefore I am." We defend our feelings, argue that our feelings are facts, and believe with conviction they are real: "Don't try to convince me otherwise; I feel the way I feel!"

In the Plaza of Water, you can begin to sense the difference between the self that flows—moves like water—and the conditions that you're moving through. We discover our emotions are like weather patterns: clouds and storms. For example, we've all lost someone dear to us. From your experience of the death of someone you truly love and were very close to, you may have been overtaken by the weather system of grief. In that state, as they say, "The rain will fall." At some point, after a while, the sun comes out again and there is a beautiful day. Then, unexpectedly, you're overtaken again by a flash flood, and the cycle repeats.

In the Plaza of Water, you discover the emotions are a weather system which the flow of life moves through. Ultimately, the gift of the Plaza of Water is to drop your misidentification that you are a victim, and that your emotions are the legitimate response to difficulties. The opportunity in the Plaza of Water is to identify yourself with the truth of who you are. Then emotions become the upwelling of life flowing through you like a ceremonial baptism—cleansing, clearing, and washing you through and through with the deep waters of wisdom.

Gini

It is important to be able to distinguish whether an emotion comes from fear or love. Most people hear the word *fear* and they think of something that is really specific and challenging. But all of those things—shame, resentment, guilt, envy, and procrastination—fall under the umbrella of fear. The word *fear* describes an absence of love that forms a limited and often crippling point of view.

As humans, it is part of our human design to have fear. If I am alone in the woods and I see a bear, it is healthy to have a physiological and emotional response. In that instance, the fear is good, productive, and life serving. However, if I drive by a wooded area and become panicked with the thought of being attacked by a bear in the woods, that version of fear is unnecessary, unproductive, illogical, and certainly not life serving. Fear is never neutral. Fear has an agenda. Fear usually has some aspect of suffering attached to it as a possible outcome.

Let's get back to shame, the stepchild of fear. Is shame a legitimate emotion? Sure it is. It's also a choice and an experience. The problem with shame is that it gets into you. When that happens you don't say, "Shame is present." Instead you say, "I am so ashamed." When we wake up, we say, "Shame is present," or "Oh look, an emotion of shame is coming through. I am not shame, but the emotion has just wandered past." That's what being responsible for our emotions looks like.

Weekly Practices: Week 5

The Place of the Women & The Plaza of Water

With the transformation of your relationship to your body comes a growing realization that you cannot move forward until you have embraced forgiveness for yourself and for the other women and men on your journey. You must also reconcile your relationship with the feminine face of the Divine Mystery, the Sacred Mother.

> **Suggestion:**
> **Listen to Dreaming Heaven Meditation 4, Plaza of Water:**
> SEE PAGE 175 of this JourneyBook for instructions on how to download your prepaid copy of *Meditations for Dreaming Heaven*

Activation 1: Forgiveness

Make a list of those who have threatened your self-worth or well-being.

Feel, envision, or imagine approaching each person you would like to forgive. Look them in the eye, and, from your heart, let them know it is your deepest desire to forgive them. Keep in mind that you are not offering approval for any inappropriate behavior—you are taking back the power and energy you've lost by staying attached to the story over time.

Find a mirror. Look into your own eyes and ask for forgiveness for your self-judgment, self-sabotage, and all the places you've abandoned yourself. It's over now, and you can release the story once and for all.

*If you are in a Dreaming Heaven Group, allow each member of the group to pair up and take turns saying the following to each other:

"On behalf of all people who have ever harmed you, ignored you, or treated you with less than the respect you deserved, please accept my apology. Please forgive me for any harm this caused you and for the ripple effect this has perpetuated in your life. On behalf of all those who have hurt you, please receive my prayer that you will experience your wholeness and perfection. Please know that you are a child of Creation—heir to all the love, richness, and beauty of this world."

Activation 2: Reconciliation with the Sacred Mother

Find a private, quiet place of natural beauty where you feel invited to do this ceremony. Invite the Sacred Mother to come into your awareness. In Her presence, experience your longing for Her nurturing care. In your longing you will find the pain and the sense of not getting what you needed that you experienced when your physical mother could not effectively be present for you.

It may seem counter-intuitive that the path to the Sacred Mother is through your distress, but as you sit with this discomfort, the awareness will grow within you that you are here to release this pain forever and to reopen your heart. With this knowing, finally drop your feeling of abandonment, disconnection, guilt, and shame and deeply forgive your human mother, remembering that she, too, is a child of Creation in a long line of children who did not get their needs met from their human mothers.

Now, return your focus to the presence of the Sacred Mother. Breathe in her wisdom, and exhale forgiveness for your mother. Then, breathe in her wisdom and forgiveness for your own self-abandonment. Release your distress and open your heart, breath by breath. Allow yourself to deepen in waves of beauty and forgiveness. Here, in the very deepest place within you, see that the Sacred Mother has always been with you. You were never alone. You were never abandoned. Her Love has always been with you, but you did not have the eyes to see. Take the vision of this ceremony with you forever, with awareness of and gratitude for the Sacred Mother's presence within your own heart.

Activation 3: Immersion Excursion

Often we are afraid to fully express our emotions for fear of being overwhelmed and washed away. We are afraid that there may be no end to the feeling, so we contract and keep the feeling stuck inside ourselves. However, emotions have a beginning, middle, and end. Experience this by doing the following:

In a pool, bathtub, or shower, immerse yourself in water.

Feel the water move around you like emotions moving through you.

Focus on your heart center and the way it feels with your current emotion/s. Notice the wave of your emotions as they move through your heart.

Imagine fear-based emotions being washed and cleansed through your heart.

Once you are out of the water, write down what it felt like to let emotions and feelings move through you and run their course . . . just like a bath or a shower. As you witnessed, if you are not afraid to feel emotions and do not resist them, they move through without restriction.

Book of Dreams Journaling Prompts

Throughout the week, journal your answers to the following questions:

Who do you need to forgive in order to return to your authentic, peaceful nature?

How does remaining in a state of non-forgiveness take a toll on your energy, power, efficiency, and ability to live with an open heart?

What would you need to give up in order to forgive what seems most unforgivable?

What do you stand to gain if you release un-forgiveness?

How much sway do you give your emotions?

Do you overly indulge or shut down in order to not feel?

What would your life look like if you let your emotions flow in a natural way?

What would your life look/feel/be like if you had emotions without them having you?

Contemplation: Flowing with the Current of Life

Take some deep breaths, and as you do, become aware of the river of life running through your veins, through your breath, through the energy all around you. Become aware of the river of life flowing from you back to the source from which it has come. With each breath, drop your struggle and resistance and dive into the current of life. Imagine or feel that you are now flowing gracefully and magically with the force of the river in perfect surrender. As you float with the river, remember, there is no place to go, no goal to attain, and no outer sign to receive as proof that you are doing it right. Feel the exhilaration of simply letting go and flowing with the natural current of life.

Affirmation

I forgive myself and all others for absolutely everything and choose a life of peace. Knowing the Divine Mother is always with me, I let go and enjoy the river of life as it flows through me.

The Plaza
of Air

The Plaza of Air

"The best and most beautiful things in the world cannot be seen or even touched. They must be felt with the heart"

— HELEN KELLER

Word for the Week: Truth

Most people relate to *truth* as being about indisputable facts or principles.

From the Toltec perspective, the truth of who you are is love. However, the mind has opinions about you and others based on misidentifications. The goal is to release your attachments to your beliefs, as many of them were formed in limitation, and to align yourself with the truth that abides in the heart of your authentic self.

Kelly

Question: *How can you tell when a blonde has been making chocolate chip cookies?*

Answer: M&M shells all over the floor.

One of my biggest fears has always been being perceived as the stereotypical dumb blonde—not knowing something I'm "supposed" to know when I'm "supposed" to know it. So, I've either overcompensated by always having a quick retort to any and all questions, or I've undercompensated by wearing the mask of an airhead, in order create a smoke and mirrors comedy routine to distract people from finding me inadequate.

Before I even knew there was a blonde stereotype, I used

to be an incredibly shy kid. It took a lot for me to open up and feel comfortable with people. I was the type to cling as I hid behind my mother's leg . . . long after it was fashionable to do so. Growing up, I'd cringe when a "stranger" tried to strike up a conversation with me, or if someone would ask me a question I didn't know the answer to. When my mind would draw a blank, I'd blaze scarlet, squeeze my eyes shut, and wish the entire scene away.

To avoid this hell realm as an adult, I've studied with great master teachers, sought answers, and chased the elusive carrot of, "If I know enough, am smart enough, or at least can talk fast enough, I'll be safe, no one will be able to hurt me."

When Lee, Gini, and Frank told us (and I paraphrase), "Of all the plazas thus far, the Plaza of Air poses the biggest challenge, because most people are attached with *Crazy Glue* to their thoughts and beliefs . . . never mind what is actually true."

I could see how, as open minded as I'd prided myself on being, admitting, "I don't know" or worse, "I'm wrong" seemed like digging my own grave (but not in the spiritually correct way as the grave I'd dug back at the Plaza of Earth!).

I remembered a conversation I had with the amazing Byron Katie about having "open-minded surgery," and how liberating it can be when we "lose our minds" and examine our beliefs . . . and then let them go if they aren't serving us.

I also know it is believed by neuroscientists that, at any given moment, there are approximately two million bits of information available to perceive. However, most of us are capable of perceiving only nine bits of information (at most) at any given moment. You don't have to be a mathematical genius to realize there is more going on in this big, beautiful world than we have eyes to see, ears to hear, or minds to calculate.

In the Plaza of Air I vowed to open my mind in favor of the higher truth, regardless of how deeply etched my beliefs have become.

Before I become too attached to this new point of view, let's see what our guides have to say. . . .

Describe to us what happens in the Plaza of Air.

Rico

The Plaza of Air is one of my favorite plazas in Teotihuacán. There's a special gift from Teo in this plaza—an offering from another dimension of being. For some, it is the place where they experience their first inkling of the magic of Teotihuacán.

If you notice the way the journey is laid out, we're moving through the aspects of being a human. We're in a physical body—the densest aspect of our manifestation—and we dealt with that in the Plaza of Earth. Next is water, which is emotion, and we discover that we're the flow, not the emotion. Then, in the Plaza of Air, we come to the next level of density, the mind, where magic awaits us.

Gini

The Plaza of Air has this huge rock in the center that represents the heart. Covering the rock are all of our false beliefs, beliefs that originated out of fear. They're false because they don't have legs to stand on for long. Love is the only thing that can stand the test of time. Love doesn't require our belief to persist.

Rico

In the Plaza of Air, besides the rock shaped like a small pyramid, is empty space. The Plaza is full of air—hot air—full of mind. It is believed that the small pyramid within the plaza is imbued with black light, the first cosmic out breath, the original "Yes!" of creation moving into manifestation. This energy is the foundational light from which the infinity of everything manifested, including the visible world, what we see everywhere around us.

Gini

In the Plaza of Air, we must be willing to get to the bottom of the false beliefs that have characterized the person we thought ourselves to be. We are going after our beliefs that arose out of fear, so that instead, we can begin to see what is true. We ask ourselves:

What do I really believe? Is this belief heartfelt?

Is this belief from the authentic self?

Our soul is our connection to the heart of the infinite . . . and it needs a muscle to operate in our lives, so it uses the heart.

Lee

Our beliefs are etheric. I often ask people, "Show me your beliefs. Show me something you believe right now. Literally, bring it forward. Manifest it. Let me see your belief system."

They can't do it.

We can see representations of beliefs as we use belief to create structure in our life. You can build a church and say, "I believe in this faith or that religion, so I've built a temple, church, or mosque to represent my beliefs." But that building is a building. The building doesn't necessarily have anything to do with the beliefs. It's a physical creation that is a result of the belief, through intention and action. The reality of the mind is that it isn't real.

Show me where it is real.

My belief system is unique to me. Your belief system is unique to you. Maybe we can learn to respect that there are seven billion humans on this planet, which means there are seven billion individual realities going on. Certainly there are crossroads and connective points where we agree on the same versions of things.

But the actual truth is that each of us carries a unique reality within our own mind, a unique interpretation, a unique set of experiences; and each one of us humans is a unique creature—a unique being.

In the Plaza of Air, we have the opportunity to look at our individual relationships with our beliefs and to look at our individual relationships with our mind. As we do this, it's not so different than what we've done in the previous plazas.

For me, the first step is to look at the relationship I am living with my mind. For example, I see the mind is a *dream tool*. The mind imagines; the mind processes information like a computer. It can hold whole constructs of understandings, beliefs, descriptions, definitions, knowledge, and wisdom. The mind is the human data processor, which holds all the information gathered and downloaded over the course of a lifetime.

However, we are not our minds. The mind is an aspect of being human. Think of it this way: if you are your mind, then who is listening? Who is hearing the voices in your head? Who's hearing the thoughts that you're having?

We're the witnesses to what we think. We're the ones listening to all of those voices and all of those characters that exist in our head. The relationship we live with our mind boils down to these questions:

Are you responsible for how you choose to react to the voices in your head? Are you responsible for your judgments, opinions, thoughts, and beliefs?

Are you an adult in relationship with your mind, or have you given your mind complete control and authority over your life and your reality?

If you think something's wrong, do you react wildly or respond rationally?

Do you get hooked by your thoughts and beliefs to such a degree that you have no choice—no pause or space between thought and reaction?

We are responsible for the nature of the relationship we live with our mind—with all of its beliefs, judgments, and constructs.

Gini

When we come from our authentic heart we are living *soulfully,* and the divine comes to life in our lives. To get there, we need to move away from our false beliefs.

Rico

Our mind is like a flashlight with a tiny little aperture. We keep moving the flashlight around, finding evidence that proves that what we believe to be true is true. In order to do this, we overlook ten times more evidence that would easily prove our beliefs are not true. However, we go past the evidence to the contrary, because the mind looks for evidence that reinforces what it "knows" to be true. This is called the first *attention.*

The first attention is what we learn to believe from our family of origin. It's called the "first attention" simply because it came first in our life experience. As children, we learn that certain things are absolutely true.

Our parents, our families, our school systems, and our culture reinforce this little flashlight beam, and they applaud us when we hang on to the flashlight of the understanding they taught us. Though their intentions are good, the beliefs are limited and can inhibit us from living the lives we were born to live.

As a matter of fact, a lot of psychotherapeutic processes attempt to help people find relief from stress in their lives by loosening their grip on the flashlight. The problem is that no matter how loose and comfortable your grip is, if you're still looking through that little aperture of the flashlight's beam, you will have a very limited view of what's possible.

Weekly Practices: Week 6—The Plaza of Air

Your pain is the breaking of the shell that encloses your understanding. Even as the stone of the fruit must break, that its heart may stand in the sun, so you must know pain.

—Kahlil Gibran

We've inherited beliefs that have been passed down through generations. We've hardly questioned the validity of these beliefs, as our minds have been conditioned to only see what they believe to be true, not the greater reality surrounding us. Many of our unquestioned beliefs were birthed from fear and validated through a group consensus like *The Emperor's New Clothes*. Here in the Plaza of Air, we can shift our awareness and notice our heart, which offers us an innate wisdom beyond thinking and beyond belief. With this new awareness, we can choose to hand over our grip on our belief system to the Angel of Death. Once we do this, we can grant our hearts authority over our decision-making.

Suggestion:

Listen to Dreaming Heaven Meditation 5, Plaza of Air:

SEE PAGE 175 of this JourneyBook for instructions on how to download your prepaid copy of *Meditations from Dreaming Heaven*

Activation 1: Flashlight

Get a flashlight (or use the LED light from a cell phone). The flashlight represents the mind with its narrow beam of focus.

Turn on the flashlight and turn off other light sources. Walk through your home, office, or backyard. Imagine you are only able to see the extent of possibility through the tiny aperture of light. Notice your restricted ability to see the full panorama of life around you. Become aware of how limited your point of view has been compared to the infinite spectrum of light that is available.

Offer your flashlight to the Angel of Death. It is an offering symbolizing your willingness to release your attachment to both your beliefs and to being right.

Look around and notice the vast horizons of possibilities in the brilliant light of awareness illuminating everything. In this moment, sense and feel yourself shift from thinking with your inherited belief system to accessing the wisdom in your heart.

*If you are in a Dreaming Heaven Group, invite one person to play the role of the Angel of Death. At the conclusion of the Activation, let each member of the group stand in line and offer their limited light source to the Angel of Death. This symbolizes they are giving up their skewed beliefs and points of view about life.

Allow time for sharing insights, *ahas*, and breakthroughs.

Activation 2: Listen, Identify, Question, Intuit, & Decide

Sometimes our outworn beliefs, thoughts, and stories can seem so solid, immovable, and permanent—like unsightly hand-me-down furniture from the 1970s that has taken up residence in the home of our mind. The following process is designed to unpack and liquefy those beliefs that once upon a time seemed too sacred, solid, and permanent to move. To begin, make a list of your beliefs about your body, abilities, knowledge, and limitations. For example, include your political party, moral values, notions about yourself and the world, etc. Once you've completed the list, set aside ample time where you will be undisturbed. Pick the first belief off your list and examine it by running it through the **LIQUID** process:

Listen to your thoughts and see if there is un-ease in your mind. If so, seek to identify the core thought or belief at its root.

Identify the belief as carefully, thoroughly, and honestly as you can.

Question its validity. Is it really true? Look at it through the eyes of love.

Intuit what it would be like to live the rest of your life with this belief. Use your intuition to see what your life would be like without it.

Decide if you want this belief impacting your experience of life. If you don't, make a conscious commitment to release the belief. Describe a new heartfelt belief to replace the false one. Ask yourself, "If I acted on the wisdom of my heart, what would I do differently?" Determine what actions you need to take to embody the new belief.

*If you are in a Dreaming Heaven Group, invite the group to share based on the question, "If I acted on the wisdom in my heart, what would I do differently?"

Book of Dreams Journaling Prompts

Throughout the week journal your answers to the following questions:

What are the overriding beliefs and mental constructs that keep you from experiencing all the possibilities open to you and the truth of your authenticity?

On what topics and issues do you consistently override your inner wisdom with your logic?

How do you find evidence to support what you believe?

Are you willing to make a new habit to question your beliefs?

Are you willing to trust the wisdom in your heart?

Where do you see people, places, things, and situations through the tiny flashlight focus of your mind?

What happens when you lay the flashlight down and look with a new awareness?

Who would you be if your life were led by the truth of your authentic heart?

Contemplation: Drop Back into Your True Nature

Sit quietly with something from nature in front of you (e.g. a plant, flowers, a bowl of water, or a mound of rich soil). Become conscious of your breath as you focus your gaze on the nature in front of you. Become aware of how your lungs breathe without you having to tell them to. Notice how the miracle of breathing is automatic. Your mind doesn't need to tell your lungs what to do; it doesn't need to tell your blood to pulse through your veins; and it doesn't need to orchestrate the movement of the sun. In fact, no one has to tell nature what to do, what to believe, or how to be. Focus on your breathing and feel that you are a part of nature. Notice the ways your mind wants to jump in and do something or figure something out. Become aware of what it says. Release the thoughts and return your gaze to the perfection of nature that sits before you.

Now deepen your breath and contemplate the notion of 100 percent self-acceptance. Accept who you are—the way nature accepts itself—without conditions, blame, or a need for knowledge. Find yourself to be—as nature before you—untainted, complete, faultless, a miracle. Thank yourself for being willing to see beyond the myth of your imperfection to your true nature. Offer your gratitude for clarity, and for knowing that the truth of who you are far surpasses the limitations of your mind.

Affirmation

I appreciate my mind for its amazing functionality. However, I allow my heart to run the show of my life and my mind to do my heart's bidding.

The Plaza
of Fire

The Plaza of Fire

WEEK 7

In everyone's life, at some time, our inner fire goes out. It is then burst into flame by an encounter with another human being. We should all be thankful for those people who rekindle the inner spirit.

—ALBERT SCHWEITZER

Word for the Week: Awareness

It is typically believed among most people that *awareness* is about a conscious recognition, realization, or perception.

However, from the Toltec perspective, once everything else has been burnt away, awareness is all that remains. In the Plaza of Fire, we amplify awareness of ourselves as an animal, as man or woman, as a spark of life, and ultimately as an eternal being of light.

Kelly

As a Fire sign, astrologically speaking, I particularly resonate with this plaza . . . knowing that the fiery aspect of my nature can warm and animate life . . . and yet if left unattended, can burn the house down.

What I remember most about the Plaza of Fire (besides hearing Janet Jackson's song in my head, "Like a moth to a flame, burnt by the fire. My love is blind can't you see my desire . . . that's the way love goes . . . "), was Gini's amazing chakra meditation that set my spirit ablaze.

I learned from Lee, Gini, and Frank that the Plaza of Fire is the place where we put to rest our identification with the masculine or feminine aspects of us—in other words, all that separates the animal aspect from its spiritual expression. With that, I created an altar of rocks in the shape of a heart to honor and release the masculine and feminine aspects of myself. The left side represented the feminine and the right side the masculine. I did my best to create a balanced heart, but in truth the left side hung a little heavier.

As I did this I scrolled through my mind's version of the movie of my life and noticed times when I had been clearly in my feminine energy (including the femme fatale, goddess, or damsel in distress). I also reviewed the times when my inner macho man, hero, provider, or protector made an appearance on the scene, riding bareback, guns blazing, into the center of town.

I saw how, in the realm of intimate relationships, I'd always lived in a tug-of-war between these two opposing aspects of myself. The feminine part wanting so desperately to be rescued by a strong cowboy . . . one who would sweep me off my feet and never take "No" for an answer. The other part of me would never tolerate a man who wouldn't respect me enough to take "No" for an answer. Talk about a mixed message! No wonder men have always been confused by me!

In the Plaza of Fire, I felt a profound *aha* take over me as I recognized these completely contrasting (some might call them schizophrenic) aspects of myself. Just like with my body in the Plaza of Earth and my emotions in the Plaza of Water, I could see that I have these aspects, but they don't *have* me, so I gratefully laid them down.

> **Side note: I was so proud of the beautiful heart altar I made in honor of my masculine and feminine aspects that I went back at the end of the day to admire it. I was in shock to find a circle of Japanese tourists standing around like paparazzi taking pictures of it! I imagined that these tourists thought my "heart" was an ancient Toltec relic dating back thousands of years. I didn't have the "heart" to tell them I'd just made it hours before. Hopefully it gave them the subliminal message to lay down their attachments to their inner masculine and feminine.**

Guides ... take it away! Tell us about the Plaza of Fire. ...

Lee

In the Plaza of Fire we explore spirit. Our spirit is our life force, our energy. We live in a physical body, and the physical body is an animal body. The physical body without the spirit is dead. It's the spirit that animates our form, and it's the spirit that is referred to in most religious belief systems. It's the spirit that lives on and on, beyond the body. The spirit comes into the world in manifest form at the moment of conception, and is the life force present within us through our entire experience of living in this physical incarnation.

When I say you're a spirit, not a body, what I mean is that you are the consciousness that inhabits the form. The real you is the presence of spirit that animates your physical body. Have you ever had a knowing that was bigger, broader, or beyond your typical day-to-day reasoning? That's spirit. And spirit communicates. In fact, all of consciousness communicates—back and forth—all the time. The mind communicates to the body. The body communicates to the mind. The mind communicates to the emotions. The emotions communicate to the mind . . . and the cycle goes on and on.

Spirit is my life force, and I am spirit embodied in this form called Lee McCormick. I came into this form at the moment of conception as consciousness and spirit. That spirit animates this physical body and has lived in it throughout this lifetime up until this point. My connection to my spirit is greater and goes far beyond what my body perceives, what my mind knows, and what my emotions feel. My/Our spirit transcends all that.

I've not always had that awareness. The awareness of spirit has come to me through my living experience of awakening, living my experience of taking myself apart, asking questions like:

What am I doing here?

What am I doing in this life?

What am I doing in this world? Why do I believe these things?

Having a spiritual awareness is a result of this journey of awakening.

Rico

The first thing we discover in the Plaza of Fire is "I'm alive!" There's a spark within you that's alive! It's fire! It's light! It's connected to the great fire of the sun and it's connected to the light of the cosmos.

To experience the fullness of this awareness we do a "chakra ceremony" (more about that in this week's Activations) to help you unravel your connection to the constellation system you've held yourself in; the way you've held your DNA; and the way you've contained your expression of light within the material form of matter.

In the exploration of your chakras (your energetic system) you discover you don't have seven chakras.

You discover you have thousands of them. When I look at someone, I see the radiance of what's called the rainbow body: an iridescent presence, a swirling outpouring of light, an uplifting upwelling flow of divinity.

Your chakra system is actually connected to a larger system of stars and swirling galaxies that exists within different points in the body. The aim of the work we do in the Plaza of Fire is to drop our identification with the way we've held light. As we do this we allow ourselves to move toward our essence to the single spark of radiance; the unique spark of life that we are here to express.

The opportunity in the Plaza of Fire is the chance to go to the Source—to the place where all life emerges. When we return to the Source, we realize we are miniature versions of the entire constellation of stars and galaxies making up all Creation—contained within our bodies. These stars within our bodies are a gift, and it's time to remove the ribbons and packaging and reveal what's inside. In the Plaza of Fire, the gift of who you are is revealed, and when that moment comes, you realize that *you are light*, connected to all the light of creation . . . and connected to all that is.

Gini

The fire of creation came together through the spark of two forces: the sperm and the egg, masculine and feminine principles. In Fire we release the energy of our life force back to the Creator. We take the time to feel the male and female nature that identifies the physical form we inhabit. With great respect we also acknowledge the opposite gender. We then build a bridge over the polarity of the sexes. We experience a feeling of oneness, total acceptance, and love with all. We then build a bridge over the deeper polarity that separates the animal from the spirit, and release the spirit back to Source. With the awareness that still abides, we take the opportunity to reunite with the Heart of the Cosmos.

Weekly Practices: Week 7—The Plaza of Fire

Just as a candle cannot burn without fire, men cannot live without a spiritual life.

—Buddha

On our journey to the Plaza of Fire, we discovered we are not our fear, we are not our bodies, we are not our emotions, and we are not our minds or beliefs. We now approach the final release of our mistaken identities.

Suggestion:
Listen to Dreaming Heaven Meditation 6, Plaza of Fire:
SEE PAGE 175 of this JourneyBook for instructions on how to download your prepaid copy of *Meditations from Dreaming Heaven*

Activation 1: Meltdown of the Masks

Draw pictures of the masks you've worn as a human (between 3 and 10 years old, at least). Depending upon available materials and skill level these can be done simply as a life-size sketch on blank pieces of paper—or more elaborately as paintings on canvases (or clay masks).

As you create your masks, contemplate what they mean to you. Describe the fears and limitations that the masks represent or have been used to hide, protect, or provide. Prepare a fire ceremony by either using a fireplace or a safe, outdoor fire pit where you will offer up your masks to the flames of transformation. As you burn your masks, offer gratitude for each of the masks you've worn and for what they have offered you. As you release each mask to the fire, breathe deeply and reclaim your authentic energy and power.

After you finish, gather the smoke with your hands, and move the smoke over your head, as in a baptism of a new beginning. You are now ready for your reunion with the spirit that animates you. If you are unable to burn your masks, then shred or tear them into small pieces. Once the fire has gone completely out, throw the pieces away.

*If you are in a Dreaming Heaven Group, let each member take a turn sharing their masks with the group, then lighting their masks on fire. While you wait your turn, hold space for the person whose masks are in meltdown mode, and send them prayers of support, love, and authenticity.

Activation 2: Spark of Light

Find a place in the sun where you can lie undisturbed and rest comfortably. Direct your attention to your breath. Breathe in peace. As you exhale, breathe out your concerns, so you can become fully present and consciously explore the Great Fire of Creation within you. As you deepen into your peace, know you are ready to discover your true essence. Begin by surrendering your attachment to your gender. Do this with full gratitude for the experience of your gender, then become willing to release your identity with it . . . seeing your gender as simply an aspect of the miracle of your birth. See that it came from the union of the sperm and the egg, and it is no longer of any use to you in this moment.

Now, use your imagination to build a bridge across the polarity that separates the sexes, creating a place of total acceptance of your humanity. Allow yourself to feel acceptance of yourself and great gratitude for the gift of life. Then, so you can explore even more deeply, imagine building a bridge over the deep polarity that separates the animal from the divine. Visualize a silver cord emanating from your body, going down, and anchoring your human heart to the heart of

Mother Earth.

While engaging your imagination, picture another silver cord going out through the heavens to the heart of the cosmos. Strengthen your focus on your breath, and use it to release your attachment to your life force by visualizing the release of your chakras, one by one, out through the crown and up the cord to the heart of Creation. Take all the time you need to become willing to release these forces.

Finally, as you surrender your root chakra and release the cord that anchors your energetic body to your physical body, you may become aware of a miracle: your eternal essence. In this moment allow yourself to become acquainted, perhaps for the first time, with who you really are: the unique spark of pure spirit that animates you. Cherish this moment, however it reveals itself to you, and let its message expand indelibly throughout your consciousness. Now feel or imagine a gentle tug through the silver cord. Realizing your heart is still longing to continue your earthly adventure. Gently slide back down the silver cord into your human form. Breathe deeply and take your time. Wiggle your fingers and toes. Feel the grounding support of Mother Earth beneath you.

*If you are in a Dreaming Heaven Group, play the guided meditation that accompanies this section aloud so the entire group can share this experience.

Book of Dreams Journaling Prompts

Throughout the week, make note in your journal of the false selves you identify yourself with. The more detailed the description, the more easily you will be able to spot and avoid becoming ensnared in their limitations again.

Journal about the instances you've noticed this week where you've found yourself acting out a habitual pattern of identification. Rather than becoming self-critical and dismayed by the appearance of these patterns, practice becoming supportive of your increased ability to spot habitual responses. What are these habitual responses?

Make note of instances where your first response has been to move away from identification with a limiting identity or a position.

Take note of instances where you chose to act with awareness instead of reacting habitually from an identity structure.

Describe the unique spark of Creation you are *really*.

Contemplation: Inner Critic to Warrior Ally

Breathe deeply. As you continue breathing, feel yourself at the place of your eternal essence. Call forth your inner critic. Extend your love and gratitude toward your inner critic, as it has worked very hard at seeing all that could be wrong in an attempt to protect you. Thank the critic for his efforts and let it know you are now putting aside your fear and finding you are now safe, and there is no need for its former job.

Inform your inner critic that because it has stuck with you all this time, you are promoting it to a new job, with a new title: Warrior Ally. As your Warrior Ally, it will accompany you on the high road of your expansion and will be responsible for mastering your new perception. This new job is just as busy and detail oriented as the previous one, but much more fun, and, as the job duties are perfected, it will offer more leisure time for R&R.

The Warrior Ally will now use that same heightened awareness, developed over the years, to look for opportunities for self-acceptance and love. When limiting habits and habitual behaviors arise, gently remind your Warrior Ally that you are safe, and it can keep its focus on its new job. Each time the Warrior Ally apprehends a limiting thought or action, it is an act of self-love. Each little act adds to a whole and to the strength of the Warrior Ally, giving the position an even stronger influence.

Side note: The word Warrior in this context refers to an aspect of oneself that is vigilant, purposeful, and resourceful in the struggle to overcome the self-inflicted limitations of mistaken identities. This "warrior" is peaceful but relentless in being the ally we invite to aid us in our journey to the authentic self.

Affirmation

With each breath I take, I step away from my mistaken identities and fully align with my authentic self so that I may live the life I was born to live.

The Plaza of
Recollection

The Plaza of Recollection

For attractive lips, speak words of kindness;
for lovely eyes, seek out the good in people;
for poise, walk with the knowledge that you never walk alone.

—Sam Levenson

Word for the Week: Trust

I will assert that most of us think of *trust* as belief in something or someone's word, deed, or character. And for most of us, our egos tell us we are not safe if we let go and simply trust life.

But the Toltecs believe, however, that if we are eternal, then the ego's fear based perspective is incorrect.

When we realize our immortality, we can release the ego's dominion over us and trust life on life's terms.

Kelly

Sometimes the best way to see what's in front of our face is to close our outer eyes and perceive with our inner eyes. Just as people who have lost their sense of sight are able to develop sharper acuity with their other senses, in the Plaza of Recollection, we explore the world and review our lives with our eyes closed . . . in order to truly see.

I experienced great joy in the Plaza of Recollection. As I walked across it, from one end to the other, in the dark, I felt an invisible umbilical chord connecting me to the opposite end of the Plaza. As I was walking toward my destination, out of nowhere I felt Carlos, a gentleman from our group, take my arms and dance me across the plaza. I instinctively felt he was leading me off course . . . and I tried to nudge him to straighten out, to no avail. Because I had just released my masculine and feminine, I didn't feel the need to "out alpha" him to get him to straighten out . . . nor did I feel discouraged because he wasn't "saving" me and helping make the journey more efficient or direct. Instead, I just laughed and flowed (which I suppose was still a feminine thing to do . . . but it didn't feel like a damsel-in-distress . . . so I went with it). As we walked and danced, I reflected on the journey thus far, and as instructed, engaged my intent to propel myself past the point of no return.

As it turned out, I was right about us being *waaaaaaaaaaay* off course. However, there was a feeling of levity and enjoyment in the process . . . so who cares that we were the last ones in our group to arrive at the end of the plaza! Like the prodigal son and daughter, with smiles on our faces, having been the source of some much-needed comic relief for our group, we got there eventually.

With that in mind, close your eyes (well, open them if you must to be able to read) . . . and let your guides take it from here. . . .

What does the Plaza of Recollection symbolize?

Gini

For me, the Plaza of Recollection has come to symbolize the place where we move into the deepest surrender and trust. It is here that we have the opportunity to surrender to the fact that we are in cahoots with the infinite—whether or not we recognize it. This relationship is going on at all times, but when we try to control our lives we exclude the extraordinary from the party.

There are two aspects of trust. One aspect is to trust ourselves, in ways we've never imagined. And the other is to trust the Infinite while knowing we are in alignment with it.

When we go into the Plaza of Recollection, we walk through it with eyes closed. However, there are a couple of things we do to prepare.

Developing your physical awareness is key. For example, pay

attention to which direction the wind is coming from. Where is the sun in relation to your physical body? Can you hear the sounds of nature around you? Can you hear the birds, wind rustling the trees, or insects buzzing by?

The goal is for your awareness to become stronger and stronger, so that you can make this great walk of trust. To do this you can't go in blindly, as the exercise suggests. You go in armed with a new orientation of your physical/emotional/spiritual being on the planet. In order to do this, you must deepen your relationship to what is going on around you and your relationship to what is going on inside you. The walk of trust reestablishes your trust in yourself, the world around you, and the cosmos.

Lee

The Plaza of Recollection is the place where we come to when we're in a process of transformation or change. You've worked your way through the plazas of the body/earth, emotions/water, mind/air, and spirit/fire. And now you come to this space where you've really moved as far as you can within the confines of this space and time.

At the boarder of the limits of our human experience, there is a tendency to regress—to look back and revisit old feelings. But you don't this time. This time you move forward . . . blindfolded.

Rico

At this point, we recognize that we're not our body, we're not our emotions, and we're not our minds. We now know the truth about the essence of ourselves as a spark of Light connected to all Creation. The Plaza of Recollection is a place of reconstituting thoughts and beliefs that have been assembled in a particular way. But doing it in such a way that it no longer cloaks us and contains us in darkness. Here we have an opportunity to gather the various aspects of our personalities up to the point that we recognized ourselves as beings of light.

Lee

Typically, when you reach the edge of what you know, you are susceptible to being drawn back to what's familiar. The Plaza of Recollection is the place to acknowledge this is part of our humanity— the desire to turn back.

In the Plaza of Recollection, we acknowledge the tendency to draw back, but we engage our intent to recreate our relationships, beginning with ourselves. We also have the opportunity to recreate the nature of our relationship with our physical form, with our mind, with our emotions, and with our spirit. Any time we intentionally recreate a relationship, there's always a history, a story, and a past that will come along for the ride. It's not about forgetting the past. The goal is, however, to take what you know and deliberately direct your awareness to where you want it to go in the present.

This causes us to reexamine the agreements we hold about life. We move into the wounded aspects of ourselves and release the energy that keeps us *attached* to our stories. As you move deeper and deeper into the process, your stories will come up, and memories will arise, but there won't be any energy there. The stories will no longer hold power over you.

On one level recollection is about revisiting what we know, where we've been, and what's familiar to us. On another level, recollection is about seeing with our eyes closed.

After crossing the Plaza of Recollection, with eyes closed, you come to the end. When you hit the steps, you open your eyes and know that you've made it. You've made it through no man's land. You've made it through the unknown.

Then you're on the final stretch of the Avenue of the Dead, the stretch that runs from the end of the Plaza of Recollection all the way to the Pyramid of the Moon. If you turn around, you see the avenue leading toward the Temple of Quetzalcoatl where you began the journey. It is easy to see that all the plazas were created in an ascending order:

The Plaza of Quetzalcoatl was the beginning.

As you climb the steps into the Plaza of Earth, you ascend one level.

Then as you climb from Earth into Plaza of Water, you ascend another level. And then from Water to the Plaza of Air, you ascend another level.

From Air to the Plaza of Fire, you ascend another level.

From Fire to the Plaza of Recollection, you ascend yet another level.

Each time you move into a process and let go of your attachments to the way things are supposed to be, you let go of the identification to your story, your memories, your history, and your judgment.

As you let go, you begin to lighten up, literally and energetically, and you begin to ascend.

By the time you hit the end of the Plaza of Recollection and you step up on the Avenue again, it's a clear, straight shot to the Pyramid of the Moon. This is where the walk to the Pyramid of the Moon begins . . . the time when you recollect all of the energy of your life up to that point.

The Etheric Double

Kelly

I'd known about the concept of a higher self . . . but the *etheric double* is quite another thing. I experienced it like my evil twin, my bloated ego filled with hot air, self-importance, and pomp and circumstance.

Normally I like to keep my ego—and all that comes along with it—in check, neatly tucked into my inner closet. But this exercise was about allowing all my self-importance to be revealed in plain sight. Counter instinctual, I know. Not something you think you are going to do on a spiritual journey . . . but hey, when in Teotihuacán . . .

Letting my etheric double out of the closet so that she could grow to the size of the sky was like letting my inner *Cruella de Ville* run wild. As I gave her breathing space to walk in the sunlight, instead of being shoved into a hovel, I felt a bizarre inner peacefulness and relief. Brilliant reverse psychology on the part of the Toltec guides!

Speaking of the guides . . . allow them to give you the lay of the land on this bizarre and brilliant leg of the journey. . . .

Tell us about the "etheric double" and why we give it space to grow, and grow ...

The creation of our etheric double is a calling in of all the energy that has passed through us during the course of our lifetime. This isn't a conscious rehashing of all our memories—it's not like you're going through every moment of every day of your entire life. It's more like you plug into your computer and hit the download button, so that everything that's come through you in this lifetime is being dumped into the double. It's something that can happen just because we say so—because we're willing to go there, and we set that intention in motion by making it so.

On the walk of Recollection to the Pyramid of the Moon, we imagine that our etheric double is walking with us, beside us, or behind us. I picture it like a bubble person who begins the same size and height we are. With each step as we move up the avenue, we allow all the energy of our entire life to flow through us into the double. With each step we are giving our double all the good, all the bad, all the memories, all the stories—the entire experience of our lifetime.

Gini

At the point of our exit from the Plaza of Recollection, we have gone through a process of discovering what we are not. The next experience can be summed up as our life review—a final clean up of our misidentification with our story.

The walk from the Plaza of Recollection to the Temple in front of the Pyramid of the Moon asks us to bring forward the awareness of what we're not and, by forming an energetic duplicate of this being we have called "I Am," offer it with all our gratitude back to the Mystery, so we can be free to be who we really are.

Rico

This second "self" that we recognize as no longer who we really are is made up of our stories, our history, our beliefs, and our defenses. With every step we take, we invest our double with everything we thought we were and discovered we weren't; we give it our inauthenticity, our fears, and our mistaken beliefs about our limitations, along with every petty emotion and misunderstanding we've ever experienced. As we walk, our double becomes huge, invested with our mistaken beliefs.

Lee

Think of all the energy that passes through each one of us during the course of a lifetime. It's amazing. By the time you make it to the Pyramid of the Sun, your double may be as big as the sun. By the time you're three quarters of the way to the moon, the double will be up into the sky. And by the time you make it all the way to the altar in front of the moon, your double is literally filling the sky. It's that huge.

Rico

We are going to allow all of this energy to be reconstituted and reassembled as we walk, step by step. We give to our energetic double all of our attributes. We give the good, the bad, the ugly, the wonderful, the charming, the sincere, the destructive, and the constructive . . . all of it.

All of these things that were a part of our understanding of ourselves and our life's journey are now attributed to this double—to the point that it becomes much larger than life. It's with gratitude that we can do this process, because what we're giving to the double is our story. We aren't just giving the story that our mind crafted but the story held in our bodies, the story held in our emotions, the story that gives us the idea that we're the same being day by day, instead of a completely new and vibrant being. All of the things that made up our misunderstanding about our true selves are now attributed to our double, as we prepare to make an offering—a gift to creation. This process is essentially *the releasing of our human form.*

Weekly Practices: Week 8—The Plaza of Recollection

*You can't depend on your eyes when your imagination
is out of focus.*

—MARK TWAIN

We've experienced our authentic essence in the Plaza of Fire. Now, here in the Plaza of Recollection, we take the opportunity to form a deep trust with our true self and prepare to surrender the story of our limited false self to the Mystery of Life.

Activation 1: Close Your Outer Eyes; Open Your Inner Sight

Stand in your backyard (or any safely contained area, preferably in nature), close your eyes, and open your inner sight. Allow a slow, loving breath. Stand there for a few minutes and become completely present. Allow another breath. Where is the sun? Where is the moon? Can you feel the presence of the sun or moon? Take another breath. Can you feel the air lightly touching your face? Take another breath. What sounds do you hear? Feel the inflow and the outflow of your breathing. Notice that the breath is simply flowing in and out with the will of the force that animates you. With your next breath, slowly begin to walk in a circle with your eyes closed and your arms held loosely by your sides for balance. Imagine your inner vision being illuminated with all the information you need to navigate your way along your walk. If fear arises you can easily let it go, as you are now aware that you are not your fear; it is simply present. Deepen into your trust as you walk. Notice the emotions and thoughts that flow in and out of your awareness. Remain anchored in the knowing that the *you* who is observing is far more vast than the content of what you are observing.

Take a breath and surrender to life passing through you. Take another breath and surrender to the mystery that Life simply is; everything else is a matter of perception. With this new way of being—fully present in body, mind, and spirit—trust that you can walk openheartedly through your life.

*If you are in a Dreaming Heaven Group, do a "Trust Walk." Have participants partner up with one another. One person gets blindfolded while the other helps guide the blindfolded person on a five-minute walk (in nature, down a city street, or through a house). Then switch roles. Open a group discussion based on breakthroughs, insights, or *ahas* that arise from this trust activation.

Activation 2: Let Your Double Grow

You are on your way to making an offering at the Pyramid of the Moon—an offering of the sum total of energetic investments you have made from a mistaken sense of who you are. Every day for the next week, take a walk in a natural setting. On the first day of your walk, imagine someone along side you. This someone is another you—your storied former self. This "self" is who you recognize as no longer who you really are. It is made up of your stories, history, fearful beliefs, and judgments.

With every step, invest this "double" with everything you thought you were and have now discovered you are not. Every day set aside some time to spend with your double while continuing to give it your inauthenticity, fears, mistaken beliefs, perceived limitations, and every petty emotion and misunderstanding you've ever experienced.

Use your daily walk and strong intention to hold your focus on the creation of your double, letting it grow as large as you can make it for the ceremony next week. Make sure you feed it all the energy, ideas, and emotions of who you thought you were, as you moved through your life and as you've moved through this journey.

Book of Dreams Journaling Prompts

Throughout the week, journal your answers to the following prompts:

Describe the difference between your outer vision and your inner sight.

Describe your *etheric double* (false self) in as much detail as you can.

Contemplation: Life Review (Taking Responsibility for Your Creation)

Prepare a space where you can be seated comfortably. You will need a mirror and several candles. Light the candles and center your awareness in the heart. Prepare to take 100 percent responsibility for the fabled creature you've called *you*.

Review the life you were born into, the life you were taught, and the life you created for yourself from your responses, your choices, your interpretations, your judgments, your explanations, and your story.

Now, look into your eyes and bless all the interpretations that formed your "story" so you will have no lingering attachments, blame, nor remorse—only acceptance. Simply be aware. By taking responsibility you will be able to release the story, so the real *you* can emerge and step into the spotlight of your life.

*If you are in a Dreaming Heaven Group, this can be done with another person. When you look into their eyes, you are looking for the reflection of yourself.

Affirmation

I am relieved to reunite with my authentic self. With joy, freedom, and full self-expression, I celebrate my spirit in human form.

The Pyramid
of the Moon

The Pyramid of the Moon

WEEK 9

Age does not protect you from love. But love, to some extent,
protects you from age.

—JEANNE MOREAU

Offering at the Temple of the Moon

Word for the Week: Love

We all have a myriad of definitions for what we think of as *love*, from the kind that is intensely personal, to that which is for our fellow man, to the kind based on sexual desire. Mostly, the love we experience can be conditional in its nature.

The Toltecs believe that love is the only valid point of view there is. They believe love does not need nor desire lovable attributes in order to be expressed. When the Toltecs speak of love it is impersonal and has no conditions attached at all. It is limitless and experienced by the action of sharing it.

Kelly

It seems that we are trained to love "our people"—the ones who agree with us, who are from the same tribe, or who are our closest family members and friends. But what do we do with all the billions of people who fall outside that category? What do we do with the people who live their lives very differently than us . . . who challenge us . . . or, better yet, are hostile toward us? My experience on the Pyramid of the Moon gave me the experience of "being" love . . . not granting it when someone meets my strict criteria of deservability . . . but simply embodying the energy of love and beaming it on whoever crosses my mind or my path.

Ok . . . let me go back a few steps. Before this *aha* dawned on me I went through a bit of an ordeal on the altar in front of the Pyramid of the Moon. Here's my journal entry from that night:

Being Altered at the Altar

I lie upon the altar in front of the Pyramid of the Moon in Teotihuacán, Mexico, under the blazing sun, upon the 2000-year-old rock and stone platform, smoked sage and dirt wafting through the air. I close my eyes, obscuring the ancient majestic pyramids. While the breezy flute entrances me in its ancient melody, my straw hat falls off my matted hair, exposing the crown of my head to the fiery heavens above. This is the place of sacrifice, where the ancient initiates offered their etheric doubles to Quetzalcoatl, in order to emerge as their true, light-filled, angelic selves.

Lee, with his bloodshot crystalline eyes, implores me to breathe in through my heart and out through the crown of my head.

Fair enough. I can do this.

Then he tells me to do the impossible. He tells me to breathe in the etheric double of everyone in our group, and send it up through the crown of my head to the light of the sun.

What??? I must not have heard you correctly! No Way!!! This is way too much! I can barely wrestle with my own Cruella de Ville, much less everyone else's! My throat constricts, shoulders tighten, brow furrows: "How dare he . . . I can't possibly be the filter through which everyone else's ego must pass! What if they get stuck? What if they can't pass through and it becomes trapped in my body forever? God help me, what have I gotten myself into???"

"Breathe!" Lee commands.

I don't have the fight in me to balk (with my outside voice), so I surrender to the impossible . . . and I breathe . . . big and deep, each

120

breath fuller and deeper than the one before. After a few minutes of this, surprisingly, my heart opens . . . wider and wider with each breath. The cement wall of fear, doubt, and separation cracks and crumbles, yielding to a cavern of grace within me. "Don't forget to send the energy up through your crown chakra," he urges.

Feeling the lid above my head lift open, I become a channel of light expanding in proportion to the freight train of energy charging through me, carrying the group's etheric doubles. The more I breathe, the larger becomes my capacity to release the Etheric Double Express. Good Riddance!

My body trembles with an unexpected ecstasy. No longer concerned about it being too much to handle . . . all I have to do is let it ride through me, and once it leaves my crown, God will do the rest.

I am no longer sitting upon the gravel and stone, but floating as I travel through diamond fields of sight and sound, pulsating waves of unconditional universal love swirling through me.

Tears of relief spill down my cheeks in a river of awe, dissolving my sticky, tricky, icky mask of self-importance. I could hear Cruella screech in a last ditch effort to hook my attention before she dissolves in the light of the sun, "How dare you! Don't you know who I am? You need me!"

I'm suddenly a contestant on a game show given the choice to pick what is behind door number one (the struggle of balancing my vanity, pride, and desire), or behind door number two (the vast expanse of heavenly light stretched out to eternity in billowing waves of ever-expanding bliss). As I choose door number two (duh!) it becomes humorous to me that all this time I've had a choice and didn't realize it! My laughter erupts in an earthquake, becoming contagious to the other members of my group (now free from their Etheric Doubles).

To the passerby we must look like a motley crew of bodies sprawled out upon one another, a puppy pile of weeping and laughing weirdos at the base of a majestic pyramid of rocks mortared with prayers from generations past. As the flute encircles us with its breathy magic, we are reborn, in this place where men (and women) become God.

I leave you now, in the capable hands of your guides. . . .

Tell us about the ceremony on the Altar of the Moon....

Lee

When we reach the end of the Avenue of the Dead, there's an Altar of the Moon. We typically climb that altar and go into ceremony.

The ceremony begins with the awareness that everyone on the journey has with them their etheric double.

With this awareness we come into a formation that connects everyone together into the shape of an open channel (read more about this in this week's Activations). We intend it to be a channel, and so it is. The channel is for all the energy of all of the etheric doubles to be fed into the middle, then sent up—all the way up—back to the sun.

In essence, the instructions are to create a circle on the ground with people in the inside circle, and people in an outside ring. The people in the outside circle breathe in the energy of their double from their heart directly to the person across from them. This creates a great channel of light and energy that's connected back to the light of the sun. It literally becomes a massive river of light that often propels people into an experience of flying out of their body and going into the light.

Gini

The Temple of the Moon is the place where we emerge transformed from the metaphoric body of the snake. Having traveled through the ascending levels of consciousness, we can now experience our true nature. It is important to notice we did not need to become something we aren't, but to release our false identifications with who we thought we were. What is left is the Being we were before fear interrupted our human journey—the authentic self.

Rico

At the end of this long plaza there is a temple at the base of the Pyramid of the Moon. This is where we assemble our group and form an energetic container that allows everyone to work together. Using the resources of our community, we create a space where we breathe, focus our collective intent, and together release our doubles with gratitude to creation. This process is the climax of the story—the end of our epic journey through the body of Quetzalcoatl. We relish this moment of great release and complete freedom.

Lee

The ceremony itself involves deep forgiveness for our abuse of the gift of our life—up to now. And it continues with gratitude for the opportunity this magical place has offered us: a mysterious reward in exchange for the offering of our etheric double. With this, we are offered back to life as something completely new.

We're giving all of the energy that we've held onto over the course of our life back to life. We're giving all of the blessings, all the curses, all the good, and all the bad. We're giving it all back, we're releasing it, and we're letting it all go. That's the reason behind the ceremony on the Altar of the Moon.

Gini

The configuration we create with the group is an energetic replica of our essence. Within the portal that's created, we release absolutely everything that would keep us from seeing through the eyes of love. Before this journey of Dreaming Heaven comes to a close, we have a certain amount of time in what I think of as being between worlds. It's as if to say, "Here's where we've been, and where we're going is still waiting for us." It's almost like a space where time is suspended. We have this opportunity, this experience to be present without concerns, without dilemmas, and without any story to hold us captive.

Through the eyes of love, we can see things that we didn't see before—things that have been there all along. We didn't realize the choice was there to behold a fearless, unlimited view of possibility. Once you experience seeing in this way, it will always be available to you.

Lee

When that ceremony is over, it's like somebody just cleaned your windshield for the first time in your whole life—the entire world looks new. Colors are brighter; people are shining; the sun is brilliant; you can see all the details of every stone; you can hear the crunch of gravel as people are walking. It's literally like you've been completely cleaned of any filters or blocks—anything that's stood between your ability to see the truth of the world around you. It's an amazing experience.

Rico

Your sense of perception shifts as you have shifted . . . and things you didn't think were possible are suddenly possible—like your ability to see into the energy fields of the place and the people around you. All the people, vendors, kids, and tourists, who seemed out of place before, for not being on a "spiritual journey," seem to have transformed into a stream of angels of light. Everyone and everything looks different in this place of freedom. You can see the beauty and essence of everything and everyone.

Lee

The ceremony on the altar produces a knowing. I can't give you a logical explanation as to why things happen the way they do. It's a spiritual, energetic experience.

On the Pyramid of the Moon

Kelly

The journey to the moon felt like the prize for having gone through the releasing ceremony on the altar. With this feeling of freedom and peace radiating throughout my body, I was surprised at how light I felt and how effortless it was to climb this enormous pyramid.

Waiting patiently atop the Pyramid of the Moon was a literal and figurative experience of ascension. Upon these thousands-of-years-old rocks, hundreds of feet in the air, I breathed deeply as I scanned across the vastness of the ancient ruins. The plazas looked so small in proportion to my new vantage point from atop the Moon. Up here, above the world, with multicolored butterflies buzzing around, I got to experience the sensation of flying.

Now, allow the guides to take you to the blessing awaiting you. . . .

Describe to us what opportunities await us atop the Pyramid of the Moon. . . .

Lee

On the Pyramid of the Moon, we have the opportunity to fly—literally and figuratively. Flying on the Pyramid of the Moon is about embodying the experience of freedom and expansion that is your true nature and that you now have access to.

From way up here, the view is amazing; the world is a beautiful place. From this vantage point, you can see so much detail and color, feel the breeze in your face, and experience the light of the sun in the sky. You can hear the sounds with such precision, because everything is alive.

From this high place, we come to the edge. We lay down backwards, one at a time, while somebody holds our legs. We hang over the edge and move our wing feathers—feeling the sensation of flying.

At this point some people will go out of their body and fly down the avenue or up around the sun. All kinds of things happen when you're willing to lay your burden down. This is one of the opportunities to immediately realize that because we were willing to take ourselves—our lives and stories—apart, we can now experience a tremendous freedom.

When this happens, it's like a death experience . . . in a good way. You lose the limitations of being in a physical form, and you get the experience of being at one with Spirit. You get a sense of who you are as a consciousness . . . as an aspect of light. When this happens there are no words to describe it other than to say you are expansive and completely free.

Some people look at what we do and think we are all on drugs

. . . that you could only have an experience like this if it were drug induced.

The truth is, we are capable of phenomenal freedom, naturally. However, most of us have never been taught that it's possible . . . we've never been guided into it. It's not a part of our culture. It looks strange to the eyes of the ego. In our culture we think it is unnatural to feel that good and free. But in fact, drugs cut you off from the ability to go there.

We don't associate that level of freedom, expansiveness, and peace with being human. *But it is human. And it is natural. And it is real. And we all have the ability to have that expansive experience.* It simply requires a willingness to *let go.*

Weekly Practices: Week 9—The Pyramid of the Moon

Let us take our bloated nothingness out of the path of the divine circuits. Let us unlearn our wisdom of the world.

—Ralph Waldo Emerson

In the Plaza of Recollection, we formed a deep trust with our true authentic self and prepared our etheric double to be offered back to the Heart of Creation.

> **Suggestion:**
> **Listen to Dreaming Heaven Meditation 7, Pyramid of the Moon:**
> SEE PAGE 175 of this JourneyBook for instructions on how to download your prepaid copy of *Meditations from Dreaming Heaven*

Activation 1: Offering the Etheric Double

Take one last walk with your etheric double that has grown huge over the week with the mistaken beliefs of your lifetime. When you are ready, locate a special place in the sunlight where you can use your imagination and intent to create a sacred energy vortex. Stand with your "double" by your side. Make a heartfelt connection to the sun and begin breathing deeply and slowly to gather energy and enlarge and strengthen the vortex. Imagine the vortex spinning powerfully all the way to the heart of creation. When you feel you are ready, use a strong *out breath* to release your double into the vortex and, with all of your love, offer your "double" to Creation, sending it home, setting it free. Do this with gratitude. In the stillness of this mysteriously potent moment, the veil is removed, your authentic self is redeemed, and your vision clears to allow you to see with the eyes of love.

*If you are in a Dreaming Heaven Group, allow at least 15–30 minutes for the following process. Begin by arranging the participants on the floor, in the following configuration:

2–4 people seated in the center—facing out.

2–4 people seated in front of them—facing each other, knee to knee.

The rest of the people are either sitting or standing facing out, and some are facing in.

The whole group should be physically connected to someone else and focusing on creating an energetic vortex that connects the center point of the group with the Heart of Creation.

The job of the people on the outside of the circle is to simultaneously send all their energy to propel their double, up through the vortex in the middle.

The job of the people in the middle is to take the energy being transferred to them, amplify it in their heart, and send it with their doubles into the vortex. These people in the center are the final conduit and amplifier of the energy to accelerate the offering of the etheric doubles to the Heart of Creation.

Activation 2: Turning the World Upside Down

If you can, go to a swing set, sit on the swing, push off with your feet, and begin swinging. Once you are several feet above the ground, tilt your head backwards and look at the world from an upside down perspective.

If you do not have access to a swing set, simply lie down on the ground and get comfortable. Let your body grow heavy and relaxed, from your feet all the way up to your head. Focus on your audible breath, allowing each breath to release tension. When you are completely relaxed, set the intention to move out of resistance and surrender to the open, connected space of your own heart. Open your eyes, and tilt your head to see the world from an upside down perspective.

Whether you are on a swing set or lying down, concentrate on your breath. Move the energy from your breath into each chakra, spinning it clockwise. A clockwise motion moves from the direction of your head down to your left, then toward your feet, then to the right, back toward your head, and so on. Use the breath to move the energy out through your physical body. Begin to color your breath with the color of the sky, and then use the breath to fill your whole body with the color of sky. Soon you may not be able to tell the difference between your body and the sky.

Feel and sense that you are literally altering your normal perspective on life by turning it upside down. In so doing, you are symbolically opening your mind to see the world in a completely new way . . . no longer through the eyes of fear, but now, through the eyes of *love*.

Book of Dreams Journaling Prompts

Throughout the week, journal your answers to the following questions: How do you feel about creating and releasing your *etheric double*?

What's it like to have let go of the story of you through the form of your *etheric double*?

How does it feel to see through the eyes of love?

How does seeing through the eyes of love change your experience of life?

Contemplation: Flying

Having released the "human form," you are free to experience life as the multi-dimensional being you have been all along. Nothing affirms your freedom as much as learning you can fly! Lie down on your back and get comfortable—this works best in an elevated place outside, preferably with a view of the horizon (this may also be on a swing set, as a continuation of the "Turn the World Upside Down" Activation).

Allow your body to grow heavy and relaxed, from your feet all the way up to your head. Focus on your breath, allowing each breath to release tension. When you are completely relaxed, set the intention to surrender to the open connected space of your own heart. Open your eyes and concentrate on your breath. Gaze softly into the endless vastness of the sky. Become aware that you have an unbridled desire to go exploring. You feel a longing to merge with the sky.

Allow your arms to float out by your side and extend. Feel wings emerging where you had arms, and with utter confidence and pleasure, feel yourself lifting out of your imagination and off into the breeze, now soaring higher and higher into the heavens, wild and free.

Riding the currents, looking back at the earth, flying easily across the sky. Open your wing tip feathers. And now fly without limitation. Lift yourself up as high and as wide as you would like to go.

Affirmation

I am willing to turn my perspective on its head, fly free on the wings of freedom, and see myself and the world around through the eyes of love.

Heaven

Heaven

WEEK 10

So, how do you get back to heaven? To begin with, just notice the thoughts that take you away from it. You don't have to believe everything your thoughts tell you. Just become familiar with the particular thoughts you use to deprive youself of happiness. Becoming familiar with your stressful thoughts will show you the way home to everything you need.

—Byron Katie

Word for the Week: Impeccable

The typical understanding of the word *impeccable* is along the lines of perfect, flawless, and pristine.

From the Toltec perspective, impeccability is what happens when we fearlessly show up 100 percent in alignment with our heart. This is how the Masters lived.

Kelly

The first place we visit after having released our etheric double and opened our eyes of love is the Temple of the Jaguars: The place of the Masters, The Portal, and Heaven . . . my favorite places. This high vibratory experience is one worth lingering in awhile, relishing, and milking it for all it's worth . . . because this place truly lives up to its name.

Heaven felt to me like the just deserts for all of my/our hard work. Walking into this holy place, it was all I could do to keep a toe on the ground and not dissolve my human frame in an ecstatic embrace of union with the Divine.

I heard the spirit of Anaïs Nin whisper in my ear, *"And the day came when the risk to remain tight in a bud was more painful than the risk it took to blossom."* So I let go and allowed myself to blossom in the warmth of the sun, in the energy of the masters . . .

Perhaps because I was raised Catholic, the presence of Jesus felt particularly present and strong for me. I envisioned Jesus, with his glowing aura and soft eyes there to greet me, embrace me, and escort me home.

I was guided by Gini to connect with Alicia, a young woman in our group. I instinctively wrapped my arms around her and held her. I felt like a representative of the universe and all the angels who loved this beautiful being. As I rocked her I felt the whole world disappear. In that moment I wanted every good and wonderful thing for her. I wanted her to know how beautiful, precious, and magnificent she was.

Giving someone else love was the perfect way for my heart to expand beyond its limits to the love that was there to comfort and heal me as well.

Allow your guides to take you deeper into Heaven. First stop, The Palace of the Jaguars. . . .

The Palace of the Jaguars

What is the Palace of the Jaguars?

Lee

After our experience at the Moon, we step down into the Palace of the Jaguars. It's the area of Teotihuacán where the masters lived—the individuals who had evolved to such a place that they literally were not bound by any of the constructs or concepts of the world they lived in. This is believed to be a place where high beings would live and congregate—beings like Krishna and Buddha, Mohammed, Jesus, Allah, and Vishnu.

Gini

The masters that emerged from the training of the Toltec mystery school lived in the Palace of the Jaguars (a.k.a. the Place of the Masters). It is said that other great Awakened Beings came and studied there. And, as string theory of physics is beginning to prove, the idea of bilocation explains how this could be more than a mythology.

The Palace of the Jaguars is imbued energetically with a sense of all of our highest possibilities. Here, by the power of your own will and by connecting with their vibratory pattern, you can commune with any master who has ever lived.

The Palace of the Jaguars is also the place of great remembering, the place of seeing and connecting with the highest possibility of ourselves—the master within each of us.

For me, this is the experience of the holy of holies. I have seen the Christ consciousness in this place—and I've known many people who've witnessed something very similar. Whether there's a physical seeing or a merging with the vastness—who knows? No matter what, for me it is the wonder of all of creation.

Lee

There are spaces in the Palace of the Jaguars that are portals—active doorways between dimensions. To go from one dimension to another is like changing the channel on your television. Let's say on your television you have 500 channels. Each channel is a unique frequency unto itself. To move from one dimension to the next is the same as moving from one channel or frequency to the next.

The Palace of the Jaguars is simply a geographical physical location where consciousness has come and gone, moved between frequencies, embodied itself in form, and disembodied itself from form. This place holds the access to help us move between worlds, and between dimensions, at will.

The greatest gift of being in the Palace of the Jaguars is standing in front of the portal. A lot of people see a literal image of an avatar or of someone they have faith in. In the portal, you may see Jesus; you may see Buddha; you may see Krishna. You can see and/or feel this presence; you can interact with it. It happens all the time and to people who've never in their lives had any kind of an experience like this.

Rico

Masters typically don't call themselves "masters." If they had to pick a word to describe themselves, they would probably say, "I'm just a flower. I'm just one of us. I just am what I am." You have the same potential to flower and blossom as Jesus, Buddha, Quetzalcoatl, or any of the avatars. That's our design, our potential. It's encoded within our creation to flower.

The Palace of the Butterflies (a.k.a. Heaven)

What the caterpillar calls the end of the world, the master calls a butterfly.

—RICHARD BACH

Why do they call this place the Palace of the Butterflies?

Gini

Once upon a time, there was water in the bottom of this area where the people who lived here would place cocoons and wait for the butterflies to emerge—the perfect metaphor for this place, because it offers the safety of a cocoon. From the death of the chrysalis of our ego, we evoke the emergence and the grandeur of the butterfly. The ancient Toltecs would look in the water at the reflection of the stars above and know that what they saw above them was the same as what was below them. They had no confusion about which was more important, the microcosm or the macrocosm.

Rico

This place is called both the Palace of the Butterflies and Heaven. Back in the Plaza of Earth, we were like caterpillars inching along, or like snakes with our bodies on the ground. At that stage we were attending to one thing only—eating: eating food or eating energy. Consumption was our main preoccupation. Along the path of our journey at Teotihuacán, because of our willingness to transform, we metamorphosed, flew wild and free, and have become another type of creature altogether.

When we are in hell, it's like being in a barnyard; we're no different from chickens, cows, ducks, and geese. We provide eggs and serve a higher master. We're trapped in a hierarchical system that is, from a shamanic point of view, insane, because we consider the fences designed to entrap us to be a security system protecting us!

All the people who read this book and take the initiative to go to Teotihuacán have heard the whisper from wild Creation to, "Jump! Go beyond this fence . . . and you will find another reality . . . you will find that we can live in a different way! We don't have to live our lives paying attention only to feeding time and the location of the food trough."

We know that these are the primary concerns for most of humanity. However, being a human in Heaven On Earth is a different reality altogether. It is an experience of beauty and wildness that is, from within the framework of the barnyard, indescribable . . . and this transformation is possible for everyone. It is in our evolutionary design to transform. As a species, we're now beginning to flower.

In Heaven there are symbols in the wall carvings of the butterfly telling the story of transformation (from caterpillar in the barnyard, to the freedom of the butterfly with outstretched wings). The interesting thing in Heaven is that you see differently than you used to see. When you're in hell, you can't see. You're in a trance; you're locked into a nightmare vision of how things are. Yet, when you're in Heaven, the same place, the same life, the same environment is seen with eyes of love, and it looks completely different. The kingdom of Heaven surrounds us, and yet we do see.

Gini

Heaven is the place of profound acceptance and infinite gratitude. Heaven is the place of deep ease and the open heart. There is no duality, because fear is not known here. Peace reigns. Heaven is the natural home of the *I AM*; the authentic self.

Rico

Within Heaven there is a sacred place called the "Portal"—a doorway to the divine. Standing in this doorway, people often receive a special message that speaks directly to their spirit. At the Portal, what looks to be an external reality is actually an opening with divinity radiating through. It is encouraging to have divinity offer us the answers, solutions, and guidance we need to know to be able to continue living. This connection with Source fortifies us with the next step towards the Pyramid of the Sun.

Weekly Practices: Week 10—Heaven

The spiral dance was seen also in the sky: in the moon, who monthly dies and is reborn; in the sun, whose waxing light brings summer's warmth and whose waning brings the chill of winter.

—STARHAWK

Activation 1: The Spiral Staircase to Heaven

Find a quiet outdoor spot to create a spiral out of rocks, shells, or wood, or simply draw a spiral (big enough to walk through) in the earth. Intend to cross its opening to mark a permanent passage of no return in your life, moving closer to a dream of Heaven. When your spiral is complete, hold a ceremony of commitment and offer your life to bringing Heaven to Earth. Each subsequent time you are ready to move to a deeper place of impeccability and awareness, enter the spiral with the conscious intent that each step releases the past until you reach the center, where you are ready and willing to accept what is next. You may also use the heart of the spiral to ask for guidance to assist your journey. Each time you enter the spiral, it symbolizes your willingness to more deeply inhabit your heavenly nature.

*If you are in a Dreaming Heaven Group, collectively build the spiral together. Have each member collect rocks, twigs, stones, or shells, and arrange them in the shape of a spiral (big enough to walk through). One at a time, allow each participant to have their own private sojourn into the center of the spiral to receive a message. Upon completion of this ceremony allow time for sharing about what each person experienced or received in the spiral.

Activation 2: Creating a Portal to the Sacred

For this activation, you will need the mesa you used to represent the Island of Safety. Take the mesa into the spiral you just created, and place it in the center. With the power of your intent, transform it into your personal altar. It now becomes sacred space to be used as an open doorway for your communication with the Divine Mystery.

Gather representations of the Sacred for your mesa. For example look for an item to symbolize each earthly element (e.g., a rock, sand, or a crystal). A vial of Water can represent the flow of life in the present moment. A symbol of a butterfly can represent Air. Chili peppers or matches can represent Fire—the inner flame of creation. This altar represents the Portal in the Place of the Masters—the most sacred place in Teotihuacán. It is a direct link to the One that dreamed you into being.

To activate your mesa, take a few deep breaths, and allow yourself to let go, feeling the emotion of the energy of Creation. Filled with the energy of the Great Mystery—the wisest, most loving energy you can imagine— feel yourself being flooded with love, wisdom, and awareness from this higher realm. Allow it to initiate you into a profound dimension of love.

Remember this feeling, for it is yours always. When you are ready, offer all your gratitude and place something in the center of your mesa to remind you of the gift of love you have given yourself today and over the past ten weeks, something to remind you that you chose, step by step, to take this journey to the truth of yourself.

*If you are in a Dreaming Heaven Group, conduct this ceremony to activate your capacity to dream heaven into every moment by carefully folding your mesa, and leaving it in the circle. Everyone stands and, slowly, as people feel it, walks around the mesa or through the spiral (depending upon what you've created), and exits when complete.

With this ceremony, the distinction between "ceremony" and "normal life" is dissolved. Life is ceremony and celebration. The "portal" is wherever we look. Here, passing through the center of the circle, a smile, a gesture, a moment of silence—it all becomes our celebration of life . . . an opportunity for Dreaming Heaven.

Book of Dreams Journaling Prompts

Throughout the week, journal your answers to the following questions:

I have a body, but if I am not my body, then what am I?

I have emotions, but if I am not my feelings, then what am I?

I have a mind, but if I am not my thoughts, then what am I?

I have a gender, but if I am not a man or a woman, then what am I?

What would it take to live an impeccable life, also known as living in Heaven on Earth?

Contemplation: Wise Council

Sit quietly and close your eyes. Bring to mind the people
in your life who have taught you the most about life . . . about your
heavenly nature. Trace back through your lineage of mentors from
this lifetime. See, feel, imagine, and remember people from beyond
this time. Notice who comes to mind. Don't edit yourself. Imagine all
these people are now here forming a wise council around you. They
have a message for you . . . wisdom that relates to your current life
circumstances. Listen without censoring. Listen to what they have to tell
you. When you are complete, write down what you've just experienced.

Affirmation

I step across the spiral, through the portal of mastery, saying,
"Yes!" to becoming the master of love I was born to be . . . heir to the
dream and the reality of Heaven on Earth.

The Pyramid
of the Sun

The Pyramid of the Sun

WEEK 11

Three things cannot be long hidden: the sun, the moon, and the truth.

—BUDDHA

Word for the Week: now

When most of us think of the word *now* we think of it in terms of the present time or moment; the place we are always trying to get to.

From the Toltec perspective, the sacred only resides in the *now* moment. When we climb the Pyramid of the Sun—literally or figuratively, we reclaim our individual ray of light that holds our energetic blueprint. In the *now* moment, we can have a conscious rebirth.

Kelly

By the time we take the long and winding journey to the summit of the Pyramid of the Sun, we have an en-*light*-enment experience. High atop the Pyramid of the Sun, our *humanness* becomes *luminous*—the way we were born to be—a gift from the light, to the light. The Pyramid of the Sun is a physical experience, which also exists within.

Being on top of the Pyramid of the Sun, my back leaning against the back of a beloved member of our group, thoroughly spent, and yet unable to wipe the smile from my face. I gazed up to the sun through squinted eyes and felt myself melt into the light. *Ahhhhh! So this is what en-light-enment feels like!* Submerged in feelings of gratitude for the entire experience of my life . . . all the traumas, all the dramas, all the low moments, and all the high moments that brought me here. Looking around at our group, I fell in love with each radiant soul.

Allow your guides to usher you to the Pyramid of the Sun. . . .

Why is the journey to the top of the Pyramid so important?

The walk to the Pyramid of the Sun is a profound experience. When we emerge from the energy of the Palace of the Jaguars, we are in an altered state. We all feel energetically shifted, because our consciousness has been blown open.

For this reason, the walk to the sun is very important. It grounds us and prepares us for the pinnacle experience of the entire journey. Atop the Pyramid of the Sun, we walk as a group, but from another point of view, everyone is on their own. Up until now, each person has been living with their own story, their own history, and their own process of taking themselves apart. But, now it's different.

When we arrive at the front of the Pyramid of the Sun, before we climb even the first set of steps, we stop and do a grounding exercise/meditation to strengthen us for the climb.

Beneath the Pyramid of the Sun resides a four-leaf-clover-shaped cave. The pyramid was built to contain and preserve the cave's incredible energy. I've been in it; I think of it as a disintegration chamber. When you go down into that cave, you can feel every cell in your body come apart. When I went down there, I had the experience of having no skin holding me in—I felt like I'd just dissolved into space. The energy that's coming up out of the earth into that cave moves up through the pyramid, and disseminates its energy throughout the world.

The cave beneath the Pyramid of the Sun has been used as a place of healing for thousands of years. There's an energy that radiates from this cave system that's like the divine out-breath of creation. The energy there is dynamic, interactive, present, saturated, and strong. Essentially, it is alive.

A marker was put over the cave to establish it as a sacred space. Over centuries the marker grew and grew. Now we know it as the Pyramid of the Sun—a celebration and stepping off place into Light. We are welcomed to such a sacred place because we have become whole, healed, balanced, and integrated. In other words we have come into alignment; we've become Quetzalcoatl. We've become metabolic beings with bodies, all in this together with our communities. We've also become the eagle who flies far above the world—able to see the big picture—moving into alignment, integrity, and impeccability.

Gini

During the walk to the Pyramid of the Sun, you place each foot on the ground with great intention as you walk forward. With each step, you strengthen your resolve.

Our lives up to this point have been wholly unconscious. Reclaiming and merging with our own ray of light offers us the opportunity to have a conscious rebirth and claim total responsibility for our lives from here forward.

Lee

I ask people to be intentional and aware as their feet touch each step along the way as they climb the Pyramid of the Sun. I ask them to dedicate each step to intending a change in their life.

With each step you are intending to bring integrity and authenticity back into your life. On the Pyramid of the Sun, it's all about you being present with your individual intention.

We climb the steps and eventually we arrive at the top. Up here we have the whole Plaza of the Moon in front of us. We also have an opportunity to witness the energetic presence of Teotihuacán. It's as if you are looking at the face of God in front of you.

Traditionally we split the men and the women. The men walk to the left, which is the path of the feminine. The women walk to the right, which is the path of the masculine. It's a step pyramid. There are three levels on the way up. As you climb the stairs, you come to a level. The male and the female split. They walk that perimeter around. They pass each other in the back. They come back around. Then they ascend to the next level. They separate again. They do the same thing again in a symbolic replication of a strand of DNA. The fact that everyone has come together energetically and is making this walk with a single intent makes for a deeply profound experience.

Rico

When we arrive at the top of the Pyramid of the Sun, we go into a ceremony. Everyone sits in a configuration where they are all connected to one another. This ceremony is dedicated to each individual reconnecting to the authentic integrity of the light of the sun. After all the cleaning, letting go, and opening up we've been doing throughout this journey, we are now in a position to bring the light of the sun back into our conscious embodiment of light—our authentic reason for being in the world.

Once we are atop the Pyramid of the Sun, we reach into Light and we connect with Truth. We realize we are a gift of light, from creation to creation. And in this mystery, we become whole, healed, and powerful—like the Pyramid of the Sun.

The Payoff

Lee

With everything you've just experienced, it's like you are a piano, and you just received a major tune up. Prior to this, you were out of tune and you collected baggage that reflected your "out-of-tune-ment." But now, you've gone through this transformational journey and all of a sudden, you're back in tune again.

The journey is complete, and you are made new. You have reclaimed your power of choice, your power of recollection, your power of intention, your power of imagination, and your power to dream an entire reality. You also have the power to say "yes" and mean it; to say "no" and mean it; and to walk through this world and not be owned by the next opinion or judgment coming down the line.

The gift in all of this, on a very subtle level, is simply the realization that life is so much greater and so much more amazing than we were taught. With this realization your life can take on a deeper dimension of possibility, and you become an inspiration to the people in your life to see that it's possible to be more than they realized. Without even trying to, you have become a symbol for others to go further, to take the next step, work on themselves, drop their baggage, and clean the lenses that hinder their vision of themselves, the world they live in, and their entire reality.

All of this is available to you all the time, and it's your individual responsibility to be in both worlds at once. It's your responsibility to merge the conscious and unconditionally loving nature of these spiritual experiences. It's your responsibility to bring the consciousness of unconditional love into form—into your body right here and now. That's how you change the world—your presence becomes a catalyst for change.

Rico

Now your new story begins. Light illuminates every aspect of your life. You've successfully connected the personal self to the radiance of Divine Beauty, which allows for new inspiration and opportunities in your life. The issues that used to seem like "problems" are now seen as stepping-stones for growth.

Weekly Practices: Week 11—The Pyramid of the Sun

May your joys be as bright as the morning, and your sorrows merely be shadows that fade in the sunlight of love.

—Irish Blessing

Suggestion:

Listen to Dreaming Heaven Meditation 8, Pyramid of the Sun:

SEE PAGE 175 of this JourneyBook for instructions on how to download your prepaid copy of *Meditations from Dreaming Heaven*

Activation 1: Conscious Rebirth

Note: If you have sensitive eyes, you can do this exercise with the aid of sunglasses or with closed eyes. Find a place of solitude on a sunny day, so that you can have a sacred communion with the sun and step into *the Light*. Use your imagination to open and activate your pineal gland (a tiny, pine-cone-shaped endocrine gland located in the center of your skull), so that you can absorb the energy of the sun directly. Fill yourself completely with light. Close your eyes except for a small slit, and gaze softly into the sun. Raise your arms and invite the light to flow through you and merge with your own light essence. As you look at the light, it will begin to splay into individual rays. Your own personal ray of light will make itself known to you. Claim your conscious rebirth, and with it, claim total responsibility for your experience of life. You are no longer a seeker of the Light. You have found the Light and claimed it as your own.

*If you are in a Dreaming Heaven Group, pick a sunny day and find an open, private area where this sacred ceremony can be held. Starting with the largest circle possible, men slowly walk to the left and women slowly walk to the right, completing the shape of an infinity sign (or double helix) four times, spiraling in, with the circles getting progressively smaller, until the group meets and gathers in a tight formation in the very center of the spiral they have created.

Begin to hum together. Begin reaching up, into the light of the sun, humming, swaying, and staying in touch with the group energy for support. Begin looking up into the light with squinted eyes—do not gaze directly at the sun—and see rays of light splaying from the sun. Allow time for each person to fill themselves with light and absorb it deeply.

As each person looks into the light, it will begin to splay into individual rays. Each personal ray of light will make itself known. Instruct each person to raise their arms, invite the light to flow through their body, as each person merges their light with the sun.

The person leading this activation should say to the group:

"It is time to claim your conscious rebirth and, with it, total responsibility for your experience of life. Each of you are no longer a seeker of Light, you have found the source of Light and claimed it as your own."

Book of Dreams Journaling Prompts

Throughout this week, note the changes that occur in your life circumstances—particularly situations that seem to present themselves as problems or areas of distress. Allow yourself to illuminate the circumstances, taking 100 percent responsibility for them as your creation, and journal about them.

Take note of the people and events that simply delight you. Begin to note moments of unexpected joy, of connection, and of beauty. Note how these are becoming the fabric of the dream of Heaven on Earth you have chosen for yourself. As you make note of these unexpected gifts, observe the ways in which the new story of your life begins to take shape.

Take a moment every day to note the shifts that occur in your daily experience by simply stepping into the fullness of your authentic self.

Contemplation: The New Story Begins

Meditate on the fact that your personal *Book of Dreams* has been transformed. What was once a written record of distress, difficulties, and discoveries of your journey has now become a living field of exploration—animated with the knowledge that you can shape your dream of life to be the dream of Heaven on Earth. Your *Book of Dreams* now becomes a partner to your personal altar—the portal you created to the Divine Mystery.

Marinate in the awareness that your new story begins with light illuminating every aspect of your life. You've successfully expanded beyond the limitations of mistaken beliefs and are connected with the radiance of the Divine Mystery. What you once defined as problems have now become opportunities for growth, and what you once defined as limitations have now become doorways to the life of your dreams.

Your *Book of Dreams* itself has now become a magical field of potential: whatever you write here in these pages will become illuminated. You will see that you have many options, and you are able to choose to live in peace, happiness, grace, and love. Welcome *home*!

Affirmation

I now have permission to shine in the truth of my magnificence. I beam with the realization that I am at one with the Sun and the sunlight of the Spirit.

Re-entry

Re-entry

*The hero again crosses the threshold of adventure and returns to
the everyday world of daylight. The return usually takes the form
of an awakening, rebirth, resurrection, or a simple emergence
from a cave or forest.*

—Joseph Campbell

Word for the Week: Choice

Most of us define *choice* as being related to the variety of things
or options to select.

From the Toltec perspective, most people think they make
choices all the time. What they don't see are the *choices* they can make
that are part of a larger field of possibilities. Your entire journey has
been about widening your field, so the *choices* that were hidden from
you are no longer hidden, but completely present.

It is one thing to have it all figured out in Teotihuacán—the
place where men become Gods—but to maintain access to this level of
love, clarity, and enlightenment in rush hour traffic, paying bills, or
driving the carpool back home is true mastery.

I vowed to do everything in my power to *embody* the energy
of Teotihuacán when I came home. With all my heart I set the intent
to remain impeccable and to love as the masters did, and to shine with
the wattage that would give the sun a run for its money. I thought

I'd remain in a state of perfect enlightenment as a way to honor Quetzalcoatl, Lee, Gini, Frank, all the Toltecs that went before me, who were transformed by the alchemy of Teotihuacán.

However, once I came down from the pyramid of the sun—literally and figuratively—and back to my "real life," I realized I had a lot of integrating to do. Just as in any hero's journey, the task is to *become* the embodiment of the wisdom learned on the journey in order to *pay it forward* to those back on the ranch (so to speak). Easier said than done. I know, for me, there were a few bumpy days as part and parcel of my re-entry. For example, I remember getting a call from my sister the night I arrived home that started off pleasant. But, in the blink of an eye, our lovely conversation escalated into a full-blown argument because she thought I sounded weird. I'm sure I did. It takes some time to re-enter completely.

During my re-entry I remember taking lots of naps; writing volumes in my journal; and spacing out while doing the dishes as I reminisced about a song Rico played on the guitar, a meditation Gini led, Lee's crystalline bloodshot eyes, or the way it felt to be altered on the altar in front of the moon. I also found myself wishing I had a Dreaming Heaven Group to be a part of . . . but at that point, none existed. So, I asked Lee, Gini, and Frank to help me concoct one . . . for people like me that needed a little (or a lot) of assistance in the integration process.

So, what's choice got to do with it? Everything! If you haven't figured it out by now, we have a choice as to who we are and what kind of dream we wish to experience. If we choose to be a part of a Dreaming Heaven Group, so be it! If we choose to go solo, so be it! If we choose to have an extraordinary life beyond our wildest dreams, so be it! And if we should choose the dream of Heaven on Earth, so be it!

It's been years since my last trip to Teotihuacán, memorialized forever in the movie *Dreaming Heaven*, and I believe I am still reorienting myself. All I know is, upon my return it was my choice to come back down to the dusty earth and take the clarity, secret knowledge, and love from this ancient city of rocks and stone back to the hustle and bustle of "The City of Angels," a place that, for now, I call home.

Now, for the last time on this particular journey, I hand the talking stick over to our brilliant guides. . . .

Describe how choice plays a role in our re-entry.

Lee

Each of us has the choice to decide, "Is it important to me to live this message, to now be a messenger of possibilities, of love, of creativity, of ruthlessness honesty, of truth telling? Is that what I want to do?"

It's your choice.

To use a computer analogy, this process has been like cleaning and clearing your hard drive and getting rebooted. You can now come back into your own center—with bandwidth to spare. The viruses are still there, but now you're aware that they exist and you have a reference point for how to view them. Once you've had your reference point reset, you don't forget it.

Be mindful about coming back and judging how well you are doing two weeks after the journey. Right now, you literally have the gift of being inspired and motivated about life again. Take it slow and easy. Be gentle with yourself and those around you as you re-acclimate. Remember that, although you are more authentic than you've ever been, you may appear to be an entirely new person, even to your closest family and friends.

Rico

The Journey, for me, is always phenomenal. It's like leaving our Earth and diving into the heart of the sun. From the sun there's a portal into whirling galaxies . . . and from there into the great central burning fire of Creation.

Every time I guide a journey to Teotihuacán, I have the experience that every eye opening is my own eye . . . every heart beating is my heart beating . . . everything breathing, crawling, flying . . . every bit of it is me—alive.

Then, I come back into my body and only partially fit, while recognizing that what I once thought was myself also included everything around me. At the end of the journey, everyone around me has also shifted from the experience of the essence of ourselves—

pure unconditional Love. I return "home" in love with everything and everyone. This experience is not "trippy"; it's not far out. It's the presence of the essence of life—*love*.

It's love seen through the eyes of love—that's a measure of this phenomenon. In the light of the rising sun of awareness in your life, you'll clearly see things that other people don't. You will see that we are co-creators in an extraordinary multi-dimensional universe where everything is possible.

You are now in a place of the love of Creation—not judging, qualifying, or quantifying, but simply loving.

And with love as the essence of your perceptions and your experience, everything and everyone becomes transparent . . . and your dream becomes one of Heaven on Earth.

Lee

After having lived the experience of Teotihuacán, going back home to the "real world" is a big transition.
When you go home, you're not the same person who went to the airport to fly to Mexico City.

It's not that you are a different person, but you have a different energetic nature about you because of what you have done. You've cleaned yourself, opened yourself up, let go of the whole construct of your life, and you've given energy back to Creation that you've carried around with you for decades. You've intended your life to become authentic again. You've said "yes" to the opportunity to recreate yourself, to clean yourself, to be real, and to be true to yourself.

When you come home, you'll find you're hit in the face with how inauthentic so much of your life really is. However, there are some things that don't feel different at all. Those are the aspects of yourself that are absolutely true—like the love you have for your children, and other relationships in your life based in love. In fact, those relationships might even feel more powerful than before, because you're more open now.

When you come back from your journey, stay grounded and centered. It's great to be connected with a group of people from a Dreaming Heaven Group to maintain the momentum you've developed. If you stick with it, you'll find this practice will serve you in continuing your evolution.

I suggest you practice humility to prevent yourself from jumping up and down saying, *"I've found the answer. I've found the answer!"* That's the way of the ego. That's the way of the mind-dominating reality. That's a big aspect of the culture we were born into; everybody wants to believe they have *the answer.*

Instead, you now have an opportunity to live life from a place of grace, love, and sharing as you deal with whatever happens in your life from this point forward. You now have a choice to drop the judgment, and instead deal with life from a place of choice and responsibility.

You can really embrace life again, because you've seen through the matrix that cuts you off at the knees from living a really authentic life and demands, "You'd better know what's going on . . . you'd better know who you are . . . and you better have an answer for everything."

When you come home from your journey from within the context of a Dreaming Heaven Group, here is my advice for you: when you see beauty, I encourage you to *look deeper.* Beauty is the original language of Creation . . . the explosion of beauty and being.

Let your perception of beauty take you beyond the guardians of the gate of your limited perception. Beauty is inarguable when you see it. The next time you find yourself walking down the sidewalk, look between the cracks in the sidewalk, and see tiny green plants growing there. We call them weeds. They're not weeds. Look down at them and say, "Thank you so much for having the courage to be here, to grow and to give your life to recovering the planet for the sake of all of the plants and all of Creation. I recognize and applaud your beauty."

Lee

What do you do now? It's your choice, because it's your life. And it's your business how you choose to take this experience and use it to your benefit from this point forward. My advice to you is that whatever you choose to do, whatever the next step is that you take, check in with your heart. Be heart centered in the way that you live your life going forward. Keep in mind, that from this point on, you are 100 percent responsible for the life you live, and for the dream you dream.

Weekly Practices: Week 12—Re-entry

You can never go home again, but the truth is you can never leave home, so it's all right.

—MAYA ANGELOU

You are now preparing to re-enter what the Toltecs would call the dream of a supposedly "normal" reality that you once created. But you are re-entering it as your true self, capable of transforming everything by the power of the choices you now make. We're all susceptible to the hypnotic trance of the old dream, because we created it! We forget the dream is our creation each time we fall back under the spell of believing that the way things look is the way they are.

> **Suggestion:**
> **Listen to Dreaming Heaven Meditation 9, Re-entry:**
> SEE PAGE 175 of this JourneyBook for instructions on how to download your prepaid copy of *Meditations from Dreaming Heaven*

Activation 1: Running the Gauntlet

Envision the obstacle course of hooks/traps/emotional poison you navigate every day of your life. Imagine that it isn't just your ordinary life, but a race for your freedom à la the chase scene in the movie, *Raiders of the Lost Ark*. In your version of the film, create a virtual reality where the goal is for you to test the strength of your awareness and the predictability of your life-affirming choices. If you are successful, you win the freedom to be who you really are. If you get caught, you pay with suffering.

Ask your inner warrior sage to assist you to identify and avoid hooks that can pull you back into your old dream, activate emotional fears, or tempt you to move out of alignment with your integrity.

Practice putting yourself on high alert in your virtual reality. When you see a trap coming, press an internal "pause button" to avoid all reactivity, summon your intent, and respond to the trigger as an awake, aware being. If you find yourself trapped, pull yourself out as soon as possible. Don't up the ante on your suffering. You are simply learning what works and what doesn't.

*If you are in a Dreaming Heaven Group, have each member of the group take turns expressing their biggest challenge—the one that keeps them from staying awake to the new dream of heaven in their life (e.g., a particular job situation, relationship dynamic, health, or financial issue). The group then enacts (via improvisation, pantomime, or psycho-drama) the person's challenge, so that the "dreamer" can run the gauntlet and participate in the play until they demonstrate their ability to do things differently in such a way that has them choose awakened responses instead of sleepy/reactive ones.

Activation 2: Forgiving Yourself in Advance for Your Fall from Grace

It is natural, once you emerge from a transformational experience, to have high expectations and think you will be an entirely changed person. Be easy on yourself, and know that often following the afterglow is the after-*grow*.

Know that it is inevitable that you will have moments where you fall from grace; be kind to yourself and recommit to getting back on the program.

Each time you stumble, find an object (rock, feather, twig, or seashell) that represents your "fall." Place it on your altar (your mesa), take a deep breath, and release yourself from self-judgment and blame. With acceptance and love, renew your intent to be aware of this phenomenon.

Activation 3: Creating Community

One of the most profound choices you can make, in support of your ability to wake up and continue *dreaming heaven*, is to continue the journey with other people who share a similar intent. When you create community, you set yourself up for success. You and your group can share resources that benefit everyone involved and experience the reality of the whole being greater than the sum of its parts.

If you've been a part of a Dreaming Heaven group throughout this journey, discuss with the members of your group the ways in which you would like to continue working together. For example, you might consider continuing with another round.

If you haven't yet experienced the power of being a part of a Dreaming Heaven Group, then join one. If there is none in your local area, then rally a group of your friends together and create one. Join the *Dreaming Heaven* family online or in person (www.DreamingHeaven.net).

Make a direct connection with one of the guides from this book for mentorship (their websites are listed in their bios at the end of the book).

Plan to take a journey to Teotihuacán with the Dreaming Heaven organization.

Begin taking steps to get involved with people who have also discovered who and what they really are. Your choice to participate and collaborate in dreaming heaven—if you can't already tell—will pay off profound and mysterious ways.

Book of Dreams Journaling Prompts

You have begun to see life's situations as dreams and to remember that you can choose to dream Heaven on Earth. It takes practice. Like learning to play the piano or guitar, you will get better and better at it as you practice. Your *Book of Dreams* is a place to turn "problems" into opportunities, using your innate intelligence to explore your options and choices. This week use your *Book of Dreams* to track your observations, note lessons learned, and even include creative thoughts and poetry. Add in things that inspire you such as quotations from the wisdom traditions of the world or anything else that helps you create flow, solutions, and more acceptance and love in your life. Your

Book of Dreams has become a magical tool for transformation—use it! In your *Book of Dreams*, review your Dreaming Heaven journey over these past 12 weeks and journal your answer to the following questions:

How will I perpetuate my ability to dream in a heavenly way?

What kind of additional support do I need to sustain my ability to dream heaven?

What are my biggest challenges in perpetuating the dream of heaven on earth?

When I fall asleep what can I do to reawaken to the fact that I am a co-creator of heaven on earth?

Contemplation 1: Golden Circle

Envision that you are surrounded by a beautiful circle of golden light. See, feel, or imagine that only energy which empowers you is allowed into this field of light. Become aware of the degree to which you fall prey to the opinions and manipulations (real or imagined) of the people in your life. Now see yourself walking through your life taking the most direct way to staying awake: when you notice yourself in reactivity, stop. Then, with your inner knowing, demand to see the truth.

Realize all derivatives of *fear* (False Evidence Appearing Real) appear to be made of solid stuff. However, when you look directly at your fears, you find the solid appearance to be more like the façade of a movie set. Once recognized, the lie loses its power and cannot persist. In this space you realize that your fear-based thoughts exist only on the surface of your imagination and are not supported by anything real or authentic. Take a deep breath, and rest in the serenity within your golden circle.

Contemplation 2: Monitoring Your Body

Fear is so familiar in our lives that we have to reorient our awareness to be able to identify its presence. The best way to do this is to develop a practice of carefully scanning our bodies for signs. Stand tall, close your eyes, and breathe deeply. Use your breath to pull your awareness into your center. Do a radar sweep of your body from head to toe. Notice anything calling out for your attention: pain, tightening, constriction, or an energy drain. When you identify a symptom of fear's presence, use your awareness to consciously choose how to proceed. Ask yourself:

Do I need to speak about something? Do I need to set a boundary?

Do I need to change my relationship to this situation? Do I need to walk away?

Envision yourself taking the appropriate action: making new agreements with yourself and/or others. Focus your intention on where you are going, who you choose to be, and what you desire to create.

Affirmation

Joined with like-minded traveling companions, I experience the reality of there being *strength in numbers,* which makes it easier and more joyous to remain awake as I dream a more heavenly world.

Suggested Format for a Dreaming Heaven Group

It takes a team to build a dream.

—Anonymous

    If you've already seen the movie *Dreaming Heaven*, you will recognize Lee, Gini, and Frank as the "stars." (By the way, you will also see *yours truly*. I'm the blonde in the cowboy hat who cries a lot.) If you haven't yet seen the film, I recommend a movie night for your group's first meeting, so you can all experience the film together before embarking on your adventure.

> **Side note: If you are unable to watch it together, let me suggest that each participant view the film prior to Week One.**

    If you watch the 75-minute movie with your group, you will want to build in an hour or so at the end of the screening for each person to share their feelings, insights, and experience. Besides being an entertaining experience to inspire your group about the process, watching the movie will allow everyone to get on the same page by offering you a common language, a visual description of the terrain, plazas and pyramids, as well as an idea of what to expect over the coming weeks.

Fortify yourself with a flock of friends! There is always at least one who will understand, inspire, and give you the lift you may need at the time.

—George M. Adams

FAQs

Here are the most frequently asked questions people have at the onset of the journey:

Q: *What is the ideal number people for a Dreaming Heaven Group?*
A: 2–12 people works well, so everyone has time to share.

Q: *How often should a Dreaming Heaven Group meet?*
A: Once a week for 12 consecutive weeks (following a *Dreaming Heaven* movie night).

Q: *What is the ideal time frame to meet?*
A: It's ideal to meet on a weeknight for 2–3 hours (e.g., 7 p.m.–9:30 p.m.).

Q: *Should there be a group leader?*
A: Sure, if there is someone who wants to be in charge of hosting, coordinating meetings, and facilitating gatherings. Having a primary point person is a helpful way to create stability, consistency, and momentum. However, it can also work successfully for the group members to take turns hosting and facilitating the gatherings. It depends on what works best for your particular group. When in doubt, try it both ways and consider the consensus of the group.

Q: *Is there anything you suggest we do between gatherings?*
A: Read the chapter in this workbook designated for that week.
Do the Weekly Practices (Activations, Contemplation, Affirmations).
Journal each day about the theme of the week and what it brings up for you.
Keep track of your nighttime dreams.
Become aware of synchronicities and insights that reveal themselves during the week.
Arrive at each gathering prepared to share.

Q: Can you describe the best way to structure the flow of each gathering?

A: Begin each meeting with a centering prayer or by listening to the meditation that relates to the theme of the week.

SEE PAGE 175 of this JourneyBook for instructions on how to download your prepaid copy of *Meditations from Dreaming Heaven*

Go around the circle allowing each participant to set an intention for what they wish to get out of the night's gathering.

Each member then shares what they derived from the reading for that week: breakthroughs, insights, and/or synchronicities related to the question, *"Who am I really?"*

The group facilitator then reads the instructions for the Activations.

Members of the group participate in the Activations, then share about their experience. Close with prayer or meditation.

In Conclusion . . .

You have now reached the grand finale of your 12-week Dreaming Heaven journey. Congratulations!

Celebrate this milestone in your life.

Revel in all you've learned and, most especially, all you've *un-*learned!

When I stop to consider how Teotihuacán and the Dreaming Heaven journey has impacted my life, I can see that it's weaved its way into absolutely everything I do, say, create, and think. In the moments I fall prey to forgetfulness, despair, or lower-level egoic demands, I remember Teotihuacán, and it gives me a jolt of *reality*. I remember what it was like settling my affairs and becoming grateful for my life (the tragedies and the triumphs); I remember the stones I collected and releasing my fears in the Plaza of Hell . . . then, gratefully, being swallowed up by the Winged Serpent (Quetzalcoatl); I remember embracing the Angel of Death and gratefully handing her my attachments; I remember falling in love with the gift of my body temple—for the very first time in my life—in the Plaza of Earth; I remember giving my burdens to the Mother in the Place of the Women; I remember losing my mind (Hallelujah!) and dis-identifying with my thoughts in the Plaza of Earth; I remember the beautiful altar I made to honor and release my attachment to my inner masculine and feminine in the Plaza of Fire; I remember getting lost and disoriented with my eyes closed in the Plaza of Recollection, and being the source of comic relief; I remember growing my sky-high etheric double and sacrificing it (along with everyone else's through me) at the Altar in front of the Moon; I remember what it felt like to spread my wings and fly from the top of the Pyramid of the Moon; I remember the portal to the divine—Heaven—is right where I am; I remember being atop the Pyramid of the Sun and becoming a ray of light that is part of the great, central sun; and most of all, I remember that if I choose, in any moment, I can dream a life of heaven. It's all a matter of choice, intent, and perception . . . all of which I gratefully learned how to do with this *Dreaming Heaven* journey.

Even though this was a more arduous journey than I'd ever

done (spiritually, emotionally, and physically), it suddenly seems so simple: identify attachments, release them, and become available for the divine mystery to unfold.

Enough about me . . . what about you? What have you experienced during *your Dreaming Heaven* journey? What was your biggest *aha*? What will you do to keep this sacred teaching alive in your life? Please share your experiences, insights, breakdowns, and breakthroughs with the guides and myself on our interactive website: **www.DreamingHeaven.net.**

We'd *love* to hear from you!

No doubt you are a different person now than when you began the journey. Or, more accurately, you are more yourself. It is conceivable that each time you revisit this journey you will find it to be a very different experience. Each journey finds you cleaner, clearer, wiser, more powerful, more masterful, more loving, and with a cleaner windshield than before.

As the saying goes, the top of one mountain—or pyramid—is the bottom of the next. So, if you and/or your group feel inspired to begin again, then don't skip a beat. As I've mentioned, there are several ways to continue this work (play). If you feel inspired, you can make a direct connection with one of the guides from this book for mentorship (their websites are listed in their bios at the end of the book). You can go on an actual journey to Teotihuacán with Lee, Gini, or Frank . . . or at the very least, you can take steps to get involved with people who are also discovering who and what they are . . . *really.*

Regardless of what you do from this moment forward, may you continue to be inspired to step out from behind the smoke, mirrors, and masks of your false self. May you follow your heart, listen to your soul, and enjoy the freedom of being closer than you've ever been to answering the question, "Who am I, *really?*"

Happy Dreaming!

Acknowledgments

A special thanks goes out to the following people who played a role in bringing this book to life:

Dana Walden, Tom Kelsey, Ted Raess, Peggy Raess, Stephen Powers, Rita Rivera Fox, Ed Fox, Betsy Chasse, Ri Stewart, Straw Weisman, Debbie Weisman, Julie Sullivan, Shannon Sullivan, Steve Allen, Mee Tracy, Bella McCormick, Lola McCormick, Georges Lavoisier, Dodi O'Neill, Maria and Angel . . . and the Man in the Moon for hanging in there all this time.

About the Authors

Lee McCormick

Born into a tribe of movers and shakers, Lee McCormick has always lived out loud. He is the founder of The Ranch Recovery Center in Tennessee and The Canyon Treatment Center in Malibu, California, and has been a creative force in the Mental Health and Recovery scene for over 15 years. He founded Spirit Recovery Inc. to produce Healing and Recovery conferences and Spiritual Journeys around the world. Lee is also a founder in Nashville's Integrative Life Center and IOP/PHP Community Recovery program in Nashville, Tennessee.

As a natural offshoot of his work in the rehab world Lee authored The Spirit Recovery Meditation Journal *to assist people in reclaiming their lives. Lee is the executive producer and has a leading role in the documentary* Dreaming Heaven, *the true story of the experiences of 18 people over five days at Teotihuacán. He has led many journeys to this place of power and has developed a far-reaching relationship with the mystery of the shamanic world that is present there. The documentary chronicles one of these experiential journeys in a deeply moving way.*

In the force-to-be-reckoned-with spirit of his family, Lee has truly made a legacy of his own. He has four daughters and two granddaughters and lives between his ranch in Tennessee, home in Malibu, California, and the Dreaming House in Teotihuacán, Mexico, with his equally strong-hearted wife, Mee Tracy McCormick, and their two young daughters, Lola and Isabella.

Here's Lee's personal history, as he likes to tell it . . .

Lee

I'm Lee McCormick. I'm the son of Ben. If you knew anything at all, you would know what that meant. I was born in a little town called Jacksonville Beach, Florida, where one of my uncles was chief of police, another one was the mayor, and my dad was the Godfather. When I got arrested on a Friday night, doing 80 miles an hour down the sidewalk trying to pass a guy that wouldn't get out of my way, the police didn't take me to jail. They called my dad.

I grew up in this big southern family who homesteaded in Florida during the Civil War. They ruled the world. And I thought that when I grew up, being the emperor's son, I would be the next in line to the throne.

A funny little thing happened when I was 12 years old. My parents sent me to camp, got a divorce, and split the house up. I came home and there was no world anymore. All of a sudden, the world as I had known it disappeared. No one could tell me about what happened because I was too young. But we all know little kids don't miss anything.

My "happy places" have always been the beach, the ocean, and the woods. Because I grew up on a family farm, I got to spend a lot of time with cows and horses. I took refuge playing by the swamp and woods. I discovered all kinds of magic there . . . and that was all I really needed.

During my college career I majored in agriculture, theater, music, and business. I graduated with enough hours to be a doctor. But I was into playing music and befriending damsels in distress.

Life was really a lot of fun in my twenties . . . until it wasn't. Somewhere along the line I got married, because the story went, "When you come from a good family, you find a good girl, you marry her, you have kids, you find a career, you go to school, you make lots of money, and you live happily ever after." It's a good story. I tried it, but I couldn't make it work. I decided there was something inherently wrong with me. This agreed with the story I told myself when my parents got divorced. So I realized the problem with the world was largely about me, because I was already very important. This new kind of importance that says, "I'm the one who is fucked up; everyone else is okay." We think that self-degradation is being humble, but the truth is, it's a perverse form of self-importance. You see the twist and turn?

I found great refuge in music. Somebody said, "Lee, you should move to Nashville." So I did.

A few years back, after having done my share of the global quantity of *blow*, I decided I was no longer interested in perpetuating insanity in my life. So I checked myself into a fully accredited psychiatric hospital. Nowadays when I fill out those applications that ask, "Have you ever been admitted to a psychiatric institution?" I say, "Yes!"

For several years I was a person in recovery. I couldn't even bring myself to comply with the rules of being an addict, because that didn't feel right. I thought, "Really? After 40 years of being whatever it is I think I am, it's all just boiled down to, 'I'm an addict'?" Based on my history in this life, being compliant was not something I was willing to do, so I started my own treatment center, *The Ranch*, the absolute coolest treatment program in the country. I knew there had to be a better way of doing things in the recovery world. I wasn't sure what that was exactly, but I had faith we'd find out, and we did.

Along the way, I became a member of the great Toltec cult—a noncompliant member of the cult, of course, and I have since gone out to teach on my own terms, in my own way. To this day I continue to live life as a free human being and if I can touch a few folks along the way, then I'm happy. *Vaya con Dios, mis amigos!*

Frank Hayhurst (a.k.a. Francis Rico)

Musician, shaman, and author Francis Rico Hayhurst combines ancient and modern shamanic wisdom with an irrepressible advocacy for having fun and enjoying life. Rico assists his clients, students, and fellow adventurers in awakening to the gift of their lives. He believes the beauty of wild creation—within us and surrounding us—can help us heal and can bring happiness and real magic into our lives . . . that's it's truly possible to be joyful and free.

Rico's book, A Shaman's Guide to Deep Beauty, *shares stories and lessons from over 30 years of dedication to the shamanic pathways and unknown teachers of indigenous wisdom traditions, including his gratitude for the gifts of the Toltec legacy and the mysterious beauty of Teotihuacán. As a guide to the world's sacred sites, Rico brings insight, humor, and music to every journey, opening doorways of perception so opportunities for transformation and connection to the radiant essence of revelation can occur. His home lies in Northern California, where he shares the beauty of the wild coastal mesas, cliffs, and ocean in support of his shamanic teaching, healing, and counseling practices. Contact Francis Rico at* francis@shamanzone.com.

Rico's journey in his own words . . .

Rico

Hello. Francis Rico here. I came to be in this life through my mother who was 16 years old. My father was an 18-year-old Basque/ Native American kid who abandoned my mother. This disgraced my Spanish family, and, because my mother was still a child, my very religious grandmother and my grandfather, a *Maketo Shaman,* raised me.

While I was growing up in San Pedro, California, there was a popular song: *"If you're white, all right. If you're brown, stick around. If you're black, get back. And if you're red, you're dead."* My Aunt Carmen told me when I was four years old, *"You are a stinky little Indian."* I turned around and walked two and a half miles across busy L.A. city streets back to my grandmother's house.

My mother was rescued from a Japanese Prisoner of War Camp in the Philippines. She loved the U.S. flag and the U.S. Army and married her savior, Jerry Hayhurst, a military war hero back from World War II. He was white. She was white. And in my mind, so was I. He was an alcoholic. She was codependent. I was oblivious.

I picked up my grandfather's guitar when I was five, and it was the only thing that consoled me in a world that had fallen apart—a world away from my grandparents, a tense world of military rules and regulations. I just knew I was going to be a musician, because when I hit a string, I leapt into the universe of sound, and all of the chaos and distress I felt evaporated; the world went away. The world of vibration rocked. Eventually so did I. I loved the triumvirate of sex, drugs, and rock and roll—the holy trinity—a perfect substitute for Catholicism, and a slap in the face of military regulations.

I had some really fantastic breaks as a musician. I played guitar in my room for six hours a day for fifteen years. Lucky breaks come to a person who does that. My bands opened for big stars like Van Morrison and Huey Lewis in front of thousands of people. Then, when the big bands needed an electric guitar player, they'd say, "Let's get that curly-haired guy. Who is that guy? Frankadelic?" Frankadelic is what they called me—for very good reasons.

I knew how to work on guitars, how to repair and build them. I knew what all the cool stuff was and what actually worked on big stages. So all my friends that I'd been on the road with started buying stuff from me. What started out as a part-time business became 60 to 80 hours a week and grew to a staff of 24 people, a business that did between six and seven million dollars a year in sales. I've been a millionaire. I got there and said, "There's nothing here. There's nothing to having millions."

But things changed in the world of retail . . . and I didn't. I went broke. For any purchase over $400, people began going to the Internet. They would come into the store and say, "How much is that electric keyboard? 1,500 bucks? I love you Frank, but to buy that keyboard from you doesn't make sense when I can buy it online without the $150 in sales tax. I'll buy it from you if you match that price, tax included . . . " and I did. I did, and I did, and I did . . . in a downward death spiral, to the point where the business went under.

It was totally my fault, but not in the way you think. I lost my business not just because I didn't adjust for the times, but for a deeper reason. During a time of reflection, before the poop hit the fan, I had asked the Great Mystery to take me to my next evolution. It obliged me by stripping away all material goods and pushing me to my true calling. I had spiritual gifts and talents that the Greatness wanted me to share with others. Now I am happily, gratefully doing just that.

Gini Gentry

*Known as "The Nagual Woman,"
Gini Gentry became the female spiritual
leader and guardian of the Toltec wisdom
traditions in the '90s. While her teachings
are anchored in a mastery of ancient Toltec
wisdom, her great strength has been her
ability to synthesize the universal truths of
all sacred traditions, and to approach and interpret these truths from the
female perspective of the Great Mystery.*

*Gini's unique voice has inspired thousands of spiritual seekers to
discover the modern-day relevance of the idea of awakening. She was the
midwife of the New York Times best-selling book,* The Four Agreements,
*which served to introduce the public at large to the mystical yet practical
teachings of the Toltec way.*

*Her own best-selling book—*Dreaming Down Heaven—*has been
met with rave critical reviews for the innovative "book within a book"
format she uses to tell the story of a young woman's sacred quest through
the disappointments and trials of her life to the discovery of a magical
book of wisdom that affords her a peak behind the curtains of what Gini
calls "The Magical Theatre" of her life (think Carrie Bradshaw meets
Carlos Casteneda over cosmic cosmos).*

*From her home at the Garden of the Goddess—the spiritual
retreat center she founded near Santa Fe, New Mexico—Gini continues
to lead spiritual journeys to sacred sites around the world and conducts a
lively schedule of workshops, lectures, media appearances, and personal
residency intensives as well as teaching via social media. Her deep
commitment to revealing the love and outrageous joy that is our divine
birthright has made Gini a cultural treasure of the world-wide spiritual
community. Her website is* www.ginigentry.com

The Nagual Woman tells her tale.

Gini

Hello, my name is Gini Gentry: Before I began to investigate the truth of who I really am, I was pretty sure I was intrinsically flawed. To cover up the pain of not being OK, I focused my attention on creating a great image. Image became everything so I was the last person you'd have ever expected to make the journey to awakening. I was way too cool to be spiritual. For the longest time, I assumed everyone thought and felt as I did, at least all the ones who mattered. I had no idea what projection meant; but if I had, I'd have been sure that it had nothing to do with me. I was certain that reality was a concrete, indisputable thing that in no way was influenced by my point of view. I was proud to be a perfectionist, happy to exert and maintain control, and delighted to rescue friends while completely ignoring their role in creating their own predicaments.

My idea of truth was a limited, sugarcoated version of my opinion, carefully yet unconsciously contrived to keep me safe and support my self-image. Politically, I was interested in human rights; socially, I was interested in the injustices of my girlfriends' romantic relationships. I thought events, circumstances, bad luck, or bad karma caused all my discontent. It never once occurred to me that I might be reactionary or that my perception could be tainted by my past experiences. I was proud to be a victim of life as I somehow managed to interpret that to mean I was not a bad person. Besides, as far as I could see, everyone thought just like I did.

Little did I know that I was a devotee of a broken belief system. Before I began my search for truth in earnest, it never once occurred to me that another point of view about reality could exist. Fortunately, painful circumstances in my life propelled me into further inquiry.

Through my quest, I gratefully discovered my personal history—AKA, MY STORY—was my fearful perception of life events filtered through the greatest story of my life: the lie of my imperfection. When my story said life was unfair, life had simply reflected my beliefs back to me, not created them. As my perception changed, so did my life experience. The secret to my happiness had been attached to the perceptions all along. After a long and challenging journey, I rediscovered the truth of my innate magnificence—the divine I AM. The truth about myself has set me free.

Kelly Sullivan Walden

Known as "The Dream Oracle," Kelly Sullivan Walden is a certified clinical hypnotherapist and best-selling author of numerous books, including It's All In Your Dreams; I Had the Strangest Dream—The Dreamer's Dictionary for the 21st Century; Discover Your Inner Goddess Queen—An Inspirational Journey from Drama Queen to Goddess Queen; *and a unique and beautiful card deck and guidebook,* Dream Oracle Cards for the Awakening Dreamer *featuring Fusionart by Rassouli.*

Kelly is a sought after inspirational speaker who has spoken, by invitation, at the United Nations. Kelly hosts "The D-Spot" weekly radio show where she explores the nexus of Dreams, Desires, and Destiny. You can see her regularly on television as FOX News's Dream Expert. As the former President of the L.A. chapter of the Women's National Book Association, Kelly has served as a United Nations NGO representative, which inspired her to create The Dream Project—*a non-profit educational program that empowers young people to access their dreaming minds to discover solutions to world issues. Kelly is passionate about the magical realm of dreams and their ability to heal, reveal, and uplift the quality of our waking lives. Kelly credits each of her journeys to Teotihuacán for being a catalyst in helping her to wake up and live her "dream life," which she shares with her husband, Dana Walden, (producer/director of* Dreaming Heaven, the movie), *in Topanga, California.*

For more information about Kelly go to:
www.kellysullivanwalden.com

Kelly's personal wish for you all . . .

Kelly

As narrator of this book, you already know a lot about my personal story. I'd like to take this final opportunity to wish you all the beauty and wonder that life has to offer. And I'll see you in the Dreamtime!

Download Meditations

Your purchase of this Dreaming Heaven DVD & JourneyBook package includes a pre-paid download of the

DREAMING HEAVEN MEDITATIONS (Part 1 and Part 2).

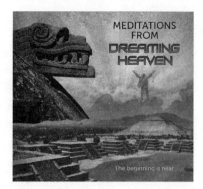

The complete meditations program is approximately two hours in length (there are 9 different meditations in all) and thus will take a little while to download, depending on the speed of your internet connection. It's well worth the wait! Simply enter the URL (web address) below in your browser, and when you arrive at the Meditations Download website, follow the instructions to enter your email address and the PASSWORD provided below. Your download will begin immediately.

These guided meditations will assist the readers on their individual journey and provide greater insight, awareness, clarity, and depth to their Dreaming Heaven experience.

Once again, to get your pre-paid copy of the Dreaming Heaven Meditations, simply visit the website below and use the password provided:

URL: http://www.dreamingheaven.net/dhmeditations/

PASSWORD: meditateheaven

The beginning is near! The journey of a lifetime starts now.

Music composed and arranged by Dana Walden

Meditations led by Lee McCormick and Frank Hayhurst

MEDITATIONS FROM DREAMING HEAVEN

INTRODUCTION (27:27)

CROSSING THE RIVER (10:25)

PLAZA OF EARTH (20:53)

PLAZA OF WATER (12:57)

PLAZA OF AIR (10:32)

PLAZA OF FIRE (12:19)

PYRAMID OF THE MOON (7:25)

PYRAMID OF THE SUN (8:11)

RE-ENTRY (7:40)

Dreaming Heaven Soundtrack Album

Packed with inspirational music!
Contains 17 original songs from and
inspired by the movie—featuring a host of
extraordinary singers such as **Donna Delory**
(kirtan recording artist and vocalist with
Madonna), **Arnold McCuller** (recording
and touring artist with James Taylor, Phil
Collins, Lyle Lovett & more), **Dana Walden**
(platinum recording artist and hit songwriter
of Champaign—*How 'Bout Us*), **Valerie**

Pinkston (vocalist with Whitney Houston, Ray Charles, Queen Latifah, Diana Ross,
Michael Buble, and many more), and cowboy shaman/Nashville recording artist **Lee
McCormick**, among others.

Featured instrumentalists include violinists **Scarlett Rivera** (of Bob Dylan
& Rolling Thunder Revue) and **Chris Woods**; guitarist **Philippo Franchini** (who
composed the film score with Dana Walden); the accordion and mandolin of
Phil Parlapiano (of John Prine and Rod Stewart); **Jim Tullio** (Grammy-winning
and Emmy-winning bassist with John Prine, Leonard Cohen, Bonnie Raitt, Steve
Goodman, Corky Siegel, and Ritchie Havens); and the singular **Joe Romersa** (the
Grammy-winning recording engineer who engineered and mixed the *Dreaming
Heaven* soundtrack album), a multi-instrumentalist whose credits include recording
and performing with Linda Ronstadt, Tom Petty, Jackson Browne, Bruce Springsteen,
and Bob Dylan).

The *Dreaming Heaven* soundtrack album is a rare collection of deeply moving and
heartfelt Americana, blues, country rock, and pop music.

The Songs
Dreaming Heaven | Another Day in My Life | Rebirth | Long Ol' Road |
In God's Light | Angel of Death | Flying on the Moon | In These Rooms |
Blessed | Sun Ceremony | Shine On | I Found | Come in Through My Door |
Shadows and the Clouds | Waiting for the Light | Walk With Me Maria |
Round and Round

Produced and Arranged by Dana Walden
Except *Blessed,* produced by Jim Tulio; and *I Found,* produced by Francis Rico

Available at **www.DreamingHeaven.net**
Use Coupon Code "HVN17" to receive a 25% discount off the regular album
price.

Other Offerings from Agape Media

Agape Media International (AMI) is dedicated to promoting artists and art forms that uplift the human spirit and inspiring individuals to contribute their gifts and talents to the creation of a world that works for everyone.

Books

Michael Bernard Beckwith | *TranscenDance Expanded* (Book & CD Set)
Cynthia Occelli | *Resurrecting Venus*
Dianne Burnett | *The Road To Reality*
Charles Holt | *Intuitive Rebel*
Carl Studna | *Click! – Choosing Love One Frame At A Time*
Michael Bernard Beckwith | *The Answer Is You*
Michael Bernard Beckwith | *40-Day Mind Fast Soul Feast*
Michael Bernard Beckwith | *Life Visioning*
Michael Bernard Beckwith | *Spiritual Liberation*
George & Sedena Cappannelli | *Do Not Go Quietly!–A Guide to Living Consciously and Aging Wisely for People Who Weren't Born Yesterday*
Lee McCormick, Kelly Sullivan Walden, Francis Rico & Gini Gentry | *Dreaming Heaven* (JourneyBook & DVD Set)
Adam C. Hall | *The EarthKeeper*
Ester Nicholson | *Soul Recovery*

Audio Programs by Michael Bernard Beckwith

The Life Visioning Process
The Life Visioning Life Visioning Kit
The Rhythm Of A Descended Master
Your Soul's Evolution
Living From The Overflow

DVDs

The Answer Is You
Spiritual Liberation, the Movie
Superwise Me!
Living In The Revelation

Music CDs

Music From The PBS Special - The Answer Is You
  feat. Will.I.Am, Siedah Garrett, Niki Haris, Rickie Byars Beckwith,
  Agape International Choir
Jami Lula & Spirit In The House / *There's A Healin' Goin' On*
Charles Holt | *I Am*
Charles Holt | *Rushing Over Me*
Rickie Byars Beckwith | *Supreme Inspiration*
Ester Nicholson | *Child Above The Sun*
Ben Dowling | The *Path Of Peace*
Michael Bernard Beckwith / *TranscenDance*

Inspirational Oracle Cards

Layla Love | *She of God* Oracle Cards
Kelly Sullivan Walden | Dream Cards
Michael Bernard Beckwith | Life Lift-Off Cards

Agape Media International
www.agapeme.com

For more information regarding Agape International Spiritual Center in
Los Angeles, visit **www.agapelive.com**

NOTES